Baby
sanctuary

Baby
sanctuary

Roni Jay

LAUREL
GLEN

San Diego, California

Laurel Glen Publishing
An imprint of the Advantage Publishers Group
5880 Oberlin Drive, San Diego, CA 92121-4794
www.laurelglenbooks.com

Team credits
Designed by Anne-Marie Bulat
Edited by Alison Wormleighton
Indexed by Isobel McLean
Photography by Sîan Irvine
Project managed by Jane Ellis

Library of Congress Cataloging-in-Publication Data
Jay, Roni.
    Baby Sanctuary/Roni Jay.
        p. cm.
    Includes index.
    ISBN 1-57145-955-3
    1. Infants—Care. 2. Infants—Health and hygience. 3. Parenting
    4. Parent and infant. I. Title.

RJ61 J39 2003
649'122–dc21

2002035244

Printed in Singapore

1 2 3 4 5   07 06 05 04 03

Contents

Introduction

Once a new baby's immediate physical needs have been met, the next priorities are love and security. You are the primary source of both of these for your baby, and the environment you create is also hugely important.

Your baby needs a place where he can feel safe and happy, a base from which he can begin to explore the new world he has entered. The more of a sanctuary you provide your baby with at home, the more confident he will feel when encountering new places and learning new skills.

So what is it that turns a house into a sanctuary for a baby? Certainly the people in it are an essential ingredient. The happier and more relaxed you and your family are, the more content your baby will be. The atmosphere is also important in terms of whether your household is frenetic or peaceful, noisy or quiet. And then there are the physical surroundings. A baby needs stimulation to stay interested and alert, and restful sights and sounds when it's time to sleep.

A sanctuary for a baby needs to give him a feeling of love and safety, with sensory stimulation when it's wanted and emotional peace and relaxation. This book shows just how to provide these things, both during pregnancy and during the baby's first few months. From keeping yourself cheerful to decorating the nursery, clearing out clutter, and massaging your baby, *Baby Sanctuary* is all about creating the ideal conditions for a bright, happy baby.

The baby's gender
To avoid cumbersome references to "him or her," or referring to the baby as "it," this book uses male and female pronouns in alternate chapters.

1

Preparing
your home
and family

Practical steps to a calm atmosphere

There are plenty of simple steps you can take to keep the atmosphere peaceful for you and the baby. Here are a few ideas:

- Get an answering machine or voice mail service if you don't already have one, so you can leave the phone until you have time to deal with it.
- Have a room—or even just a corner—where you and the baby can relax together at quiet times such as during feeding. Give it a peaceful color, a comfortable chair, and perhaps a CD player for soothing music.
- If you have older children, help them to keep the noise down by giving them headphones for their stereos or setting quiet hours. If you have the space, you can let them play noisy games in an area where they won't disturb you.

These suggestions give you the general idea. Try to identify the factors that generate the most noise and confusion in your household, and think of feasible and practical ways to reduce them.

A calm atmosphere will be reflected in your baby's temperament.

Creating a calm atmosphere

Achieving a calm atmosphere in your home is central to making it a sanctuary for your baby. When life becomes frenetic, your baby will need a place of retreat to rest and recuperate.

For babies, the whole process of living and growing is a challenge. When your baby is out in the world, being taken for a walk, traveling in the car, or accompanying you on visits to friends or on shopping trips, she will be stimulated. This is a good thing, but she still needs periods of calm and relaxation, and home is the best place for this. You may stimulate her at home with toys and conversation, but she needs to switch off at times and simply absorb and integrate her new experiences.

Of course, any happy family home should feel secure to your baby, but security is only one of her needs. A cluttered, noisy, and busy home simply won't be as soothing and as restful as a calm one. It's easy to create stimulation in a calm atmosphere, but very hard to generate calm within a frenetic household. Since your baby needs both calm and stimulation at different times, it follows that a restful home is the ideal environment, giving you the flexibility to provide differing atmospheres when you choose.

In order to create the kind of calm atmosphere that will enable your baby to sleep or simply to relax and avoid overstimulation, you'll need to consider many of the factors that are covered in more detail in the next few chapters. In particular, think about reducing noise, minimizing clutter, and decorating with calming colors. This doesn't mean that you can't use any bright, stimulating decorating schemes, but simply that you should consider which are the most appropriate rooms for them. (You'll find ideas for this in Chapter 4.)

Look after yourself

Your baby isn't the only one who will benefit from a calm atmosphere. Not only are babies exhausting, but the rest of life doesn't stop. You may have taken time off work, but there's still the shopping, cooking, cleaning, laundry, and everything else—much of which increases with the arrival of another member of the family.

A peaceful house will benefit you as much as your baby. When the phone finally stops ringing, the visitors leave, or the baby falls asleep, you'll be able to rest and recharge your batteries far more quickly and effectively in a calm and restful house than in one that is cluttered and noisy.

Safety and comfort

A cozy blanket will keep your baby warm and comfortable.

You can easily carry your baby from one room to another without disturbing her in a Moses basket.

If this is your first baby, you'll probably need to make quite a few changes to accommodate her arrival. Even if you've had children before, you may no longer be baby-oriented, or you may feel you can improve on the way you did things last time.

Your baby will need to be comfortable from the moment she's born, so you obviously have to be ready with clothes and a suitable place to sleep. As your baby gets old enough to move around, safety becomes an important factor.

Keeping warm

Although it won't usually do your baby any lasting harm to be a little too warm or too cool for a very short time, you need to be able to control the room temperature. If you have central heating, the biggest danger is that your baby will overheat, so make sure there's plenty of fresh air, and avoid turning up the heat too high, especially at night.

If you don't have central heating and the weather is cold, there should be a good source of heat in any room your baby will be spending time in. A bedroom doesn't have to be hot, since the baby has clothes and blankets, but choose a room that isn't too chilly.

Clearly, the climate and the time of year your baby is born are relevant—in a cold climate, winter babies need better heating in their rooms than late-spring babies, who will be several months old before they encounter cold weather.

A place to sleep

You'll need to decide whether you want your baby to start off in a cradle or a crib (see page 46) or in a Moses basket (which is more portable). Or perhaps you want your baby in bed with you at night but want another sleeping place for the baby's daytime naps. It might help to talk to friends who have babies and ask them what choice they made, and why.

If you have the space, you'll probably want to give your baby her own room sooner or later, but it's not essential for the baby to sleep there from the day she's born. Whether or not your baby sleeps in your own bed, it can be very comforting to have her near you. A cradle or a crib in your bedroom can be an ideal compromise. Some parents find this difficult and worry about disturbing the baby, while others find it reassuring to have their new baby right beside them. The baby, too, will find it more comforting to have her mother close by.

A comfortable chair near the bed makes nighttime feeds easier.

It can also make nighttime feeds easier.

A variation on this option is for one parent to sleep in the baby's room for a while, perhaps for the first few weeks or months. This arrangement also enables the other parent to get some undisturbed sleep. For a bottle-fed baby, the parents can take turns sleeping there to take care of the nighttime feeds.

Another alternative is to put your baby in with an older sibling if she has one. Obviously this would require a lot of diplomacy, and often it cramps an older child's style, as well as possibly disturbing the child's sleep when the baby wakes in the night. However, a sibling who is a sound sleeper may enjoy having the baby close by.

If your baby is going to be in a separate room from you, a baby monitor can give you reassurance about the baby's well-being. The monitors on the market have all sorts of extra features; some play music or heartbeat sounds, some incorporate a night-light, some monitor the baby's breathing and temperature, and some even allow you to talk to the baby while in another room.

Feeding your baby

If you're planning to breast-feed, a comfortable chair is important. You will spend hours every day in this chair, so it needs to be right. Again, look at all the options, including recliners and specialty nursing chairs (which have short legs, high backs, and low or nonexistent arms). You might consider a beanbag, which wraps around you and helps to support the baby's weight—even the tiniest baby can feel extremely heavy after a while if your arms are supporting all their weight.

You also need to think about where you'll be feeding the baby. Do you want your nursing chair in the living room, the kitchen, or perhaps the nursery? If the baby is going to sleep with you, will you want to feed it in the bedroom during the day, too? You can always change your mind and move the chair once the baby arrives, but it won't necessarily fit its new location or match the decor so well.

Baby on the move

As your baby starts to grow and become mobile, you'll need to make sure that anything dangerous is permanently out of reach. Sharp corners should be covered, and obvious danger points such as fireplaces and electric outlets should be made inaccessible in some way. Never leave any electric cords dangling within reach. You might also want to provide a playpen for your baby.

Never leave your baby unattended on a changing table. In fact, once she is able to turn over, it's safer to change her on a changing mat on the floor.

With every new stage in your baby's mobility, new dangers will emerge, so monitor each room frequently to make sure it is still safe. Get down on your hands and knees and study the room from her viewpoint—you may spot all sorts of hazards you had overlooked.

A monitor in your baby's room allows you to listen in and make sure your baby is safe and happy. There is a range of monitors available, many with extra features to monitor your baby's heartbeat or breathing for extra reassurance.

Baby in your bed

All that warmth and skin-to-skin contact makes sleep-sharing wonderfully comforting for both you and your baby. But will you be able to sleep? And is it safe? There are arguments both for and against having your baby sleep in the bed with you. If you're still making up your mind, these are the main pros and cons:

FOR

- Studies show that babies who sleep with their mothers cry less.
- Fathers feel closer to their babies if they sleep with them.
- If you breast-feed, you barely have to wake for a nighttime feed.
- You will become more highly attuned to your baby's needs, learning what every sound and sniffle means.
- Your baby is likely to feed more often and for longer in the night, boosting her immune system. And studies show that this doesn't mean you will get less sleep.

AGAINST

- Your sleep will be more disturbed in general.
- It may be harder for your baby to fall asleep if you're not there.
- You may have problems training your child to sleep in her own bed when she's older—children who share their parents' bed may not move willingly into their own beds until they are four or five.
- Your sex life will not be as spontaneous.
- It's a bad idea to share a bed with your baby if you or your partner smokes, as it exposes the baby to secondhand smoke. It's also unsafe if either of you has been drinking or taking drugs or has a sleep disorder such as sleep apnea. In addition, it's a bad idea if your relationship is going through a bad patch, as your baby will sense the tension.

Gentle exercise

Pregnancy is not the time to take up vigorous exercise, but gentle exercise such as walking or swimming is very good for you. If you already take part in energetic sports, you may well be able to continue for several months, but check with your doctor first.

Your pregnancy

Your womb is, in some ways, the greatest sanctuary your baby will ever know. However, because your physical and mental state influences your unborn baby, it's important for both of you that your pregnancy is as easy, healthy, and relaxed as possible. You are, in effect, a mobile home for your baby for nine months, so you should do your best to stay in good condition.

It's virtually impossible to go through an entire pregnancy free from stress or fatigue, but you can still aim to minimize the strain. Keep commitments as few as possible; you can always make last-minute arrangements if you wish. Canceling undertakings when you feel tired is more difficult.

If this is your first pregnancy, don't underestimate how tired you will be. You may well find you want as much as ten hours' sleep a night and a daytime nap, too. This could prove impractical, but try to get as close to what your body needs as you can. If you don't need the sleep, using the time simply to relax and unwind will do you good.

You are what you eat

That goes for your baby, too. The better you eat during pregnancy, the better it will be for both of you. You may have all sorts of strange cravings or develop a strong dislike of certain foods, but it should still be possible to fit a healthy diet around these changes.

If you feel sick, avoid the obvious culprits such as fried and fatty foods; you may find that a cracker or some dry toast will settle your stomach. Try to snack frequently, rather than eat two or three large meals a day. If you have a sweet tooth, the hardest challenge may well be resisting candy or doughnuts for a sugar hit when you feel tired. Frequent small snacks will help to prevent your blood-sugar levels from dropping, so have plenty of fruit and raw vegetables available to nibble on.

Spend some time finding out a little about the most important vitamins and minerals for pregnancy, and make sure you eat a balanced diet rich in the most important ones. If you aren't eating enough of something, your body will give priority to your unborn baby. While this is reassuring, it does mean that you can more easily suffer from mineral or vitamin deficiencies when you are pregnant. A healthy diet is therefore especially important during these months. Although you don't want to gain excessive weight, pregnancy is not the time to go on a diet.

Plenty of rest is essential for a healthy pregnancy. Don't be surprised if you sleep for longer at night and feel like taking naps during the day.

Look after your back

During pregnancy, it's important to be aware of your changing body shape. Your back in particular is very vulnerable, and you need to be careful how you lift anything large or heavy. Remember to keep your back straight and bend your knees. Don't lift anything you're not confident you can manage without hurting yourself.

Pamper yourself by putting on a facial mask and relaxing with soothing slices of cucumber over your eyes.

Bathing by candlelight is a great way to wind down at the end of the day.

Making the most of downtime

When you get a break from work, household chores, shopping, and whatever else you have to do, make good use of the time. Here are a few ideas for intensive relaxation and recharging your energy:

• It may be clichéd, but putting your feet up with a cup of decaffeinated coffee or tea is one of the best ways to relax.

• Even a ten-minute catnap can be better than no nap at all.

• Lie down with slices of cucumber over your eyes.

• Book yourself in for a regular massage every week or two (see page 87).

• Go to bed really early with a good book.

• Listen to soothing music.

• Laughter is a great way to relax and de-stress, so watch a video of a favorite comedy film or TV show or listen to CDs of radio comedies in the car when traveling to and from work.

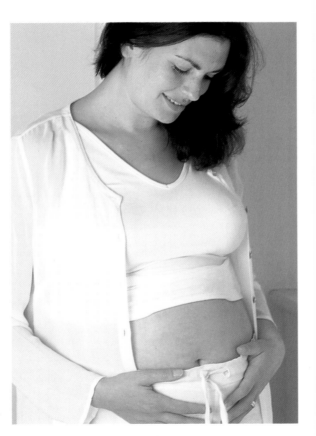

• Enjoy a long, indulgent bath, using soothing bath oils such as lavender, neroli, sandalwood, or ylang-ylang. Light candles in the bathroom, put on a favorite piece of calming music, and just lie back and enjoy the experience.

Standard medical advice dictates strictly limiting caffeine intake during pregnancy or avoiding it altogether. But, a cup of decaffeinated herbal tea is the perfect accompaniment to a relaxing break.

Communicating with your baby
When you're busy, it's easy to forget that you're pregnant, so give your baby all the attention you can during these months. Find opportunities for talking to and stroking your stomach, such as when you're in the car, in the elevator, in your office, or at lunch.

Meshing work and pregnancy

If you're working during part or all of your pregnancy, it's easy to let the time slip by without giving yourself enough time to rest and to prepare for your baby's arrival. Your moods during pregnancy will affect the baby, so the calmer and happier you are, the better.

Because work is an important factor in determining your stress levels, it needs to fit in comfortably with your pregnancy rather than compete with it. If you haven't been through a pregnancy before and don't know your body's responses, make sure you allow for that. You may be very tired, especially during the first and last trimesters, so don't overextend yourself.

If you work for yourself or have control over your working hours, try to schedule some time in the middle of each day to relax and maybe have a nap. Even if your hours are determined by someone else, be assertive about not taking on more than you can handle.

Take practical steps to reduce stress at work, for example, by allowing plenty of time to get to meetings, avoiding the rush hour commute, and turning on your voice mail when you feel you

Allow plenty of time for getting to work and appointments so you don't have to rush and tire yourself out.

need five minutes to rest. If you've never gotten around to putting all those time-management techniques into practice, now's the time. You'll never need them more.

Write appointments with doctors, obstetricians, or midwives in your daily planner. Don't let your schedule get too busy.

Preparing siblings

Us and them

One of the most productive ways to prepare siblings for a new baby without engendering jealousy is to set up a very subtle "us and them" culture, where you and your older children are "us," and the baby is "them." Of course, it's a positive "us and them," where "we" do everything we can to welcome and help "them."

The point of this is that it implicitly aligns the older child (and not the baby) with you and helps her feel part of your "team," removing any grounds for jealousy. It also makes your older child feel more grown-up and trusted. You could make comments such as, "We'll need to change the baby's diaper quite often; it's going to be really useful having your help," or, "We can teach the baby to play all your favorite games when she's bigger," or "Shall we choose a teddy bear for the baby?"

Most older children will readily bond with their new baby brother or sister.

You want your new baby to be born into a happy, comforting, nurturing world. If you already have other children, they will be an important part of that world. Clearly you will want to do whatever you can to encourage your older child or children to welcome their new little brother or sister and help to create a comforting environment for them.

One of the most basic ways you can do this is simply by explaining to them what to expect. If you have a young child, this is especially necessary. They will respond far more positively to the new arrival if there aren't too many

surprises. Tell them what babies need, why they cry, how much time they spend asleep, and so on.

The best time to adapt older children to the idea of a new, younger sibling is well before the baby is even born. Young children, however, think nine months is forever, so if you have a toddler, don't start talking a lot about the baby until the last few weeks. The older your children are, the less impact the baby will have (although it will still be a big change in their lives). But if you have a preschool child, simply sharing your attention is going to be a huge learning curve, quite apart from changes in routines.

A responsible role

Babies are generally more interested in their siblings than in anyone else, and find watching them immensely stimulating—far more so than watching adults. You can tell your older children this, so they will realize what an important and formative influence they will be on their younger sibling. Knowing this often develops a sense of responsibility toward the baby even before she has arrived.

For advice on helping your children adapt after the baby's birth, see page 54.

With the right approach, you can lay the groundwork for strong and loving sibling relationships even before the baby is born.

2
Clearing
and
cleansing

Smart storage

If you don't have enough storage, you need to do something about it. Here are a few tips:

- You can buy relatively cheap storage units made of canvas on a wooden frame; they look clean and fresh and help reduce clutter.
- If you have shelves that always look messy, add doors, a curtain, or a shade to hide the clutter.
- Things always look less messy if they are clean and light-colored. A new coat of paint on an old armoire or wardrobe can transform a room, making it seem bigger, cleaner, and neater.
- Discover where the clutter tends to collect in your home, and put a storage unit where it's needed. For example, if shoes always get dumped inside the front door, don't fight it—put a shoe rack in the hallway. If you always take off your clothes in the bedroom, keep the laundry basket in there rather than in the bathroom, to reduce the piles of clothing on the floor.

Efficient storage makes it easier to rid your home of unwanted clutter.

Creating space

You can't feel calm and relaxed if you're surrounded by clutter. Whether you have a lot of unnecessary objects in the house or simply don't have room to store the necessary ones, you need to clear space so that you can move easily around your home.

Uncluttering the house

Unless you're in the enviable position of having more space than you need, you'll need to embark on an uncluttering exercise. The best way to do this is to tackle one room at a time, or else to set aside a day—or as long as you think it will take—to unclutter the whole house. (Remember, however, that if you are pregnant or have recently given birth, you will get tired more quickly than you normally would. Allow for this and avoid overdoing it.)

Go through the house methodically, and be logical about how you tackle each room. Don't empty out every cupboard or start clearing every shelf simultaneously; complete one area before you move on to the next.

There are two main ways you can reduce clutter and create space:

- Get rid of anything you don't need.
- Store what you have more efficiently.

Clearing out what you don't need

Pick a time when you're feeling ruthless and can enjoy the process of clearing things out. Most of us have moods when we feel sentimental, and others when we feel more like making a clean sweep. So choose a time when you're most likely to get results. The items in your house will fall into one of two categories:

THINGS YOU NEED: Throw out everything you don't use, including anything you think you might want one day (but probably never will). If you haven't used an item for two years, get rid of it. (If worst comes to worst, you can always replace it if you do need it.) Discard anything that is broken and hasn't been fixed. If you needed it, you'd have fixed it by now. And throw out any duplicate items—you may need the large salad bowl in the kitchen cabinet, but you probably don't need three of them.

THINGS YOU HAVE FOR DECORATIVE OR SENTIMENTAL REASONS: The principle here should be that if something is being kept for aesthetic or nostalgic reasons, it's worth having out on display. If it isn't, then you shouldn't be hanging on to it. Go through

Baby clutter

One small baby can engender an almost unbelievable amount of equipment, and you will therefore need to clear enough space to accommodate all the extra items your baby is going to need. Think through in advance where you'll be storing these items, so that there will be room for them when the time comes. Here are some of the larger things you may have to find room for:

- Moses basket
- Portable crib
- Car seat
- Stroller/buggy (plus rain cover, sunshade, cozy cover)
- Diaper-changing cart
- Baby bath
- Rocking chair
- Baby walker

If you have space, invest in a sturdy cupboard or wardrobe to store not only baby clothes, but also some of the larger items (see above).

your cupboards, and if you really want to keep something, dust it off and put it out. Otherwise, get rid of it.

Don't forget about the larger items. You can clear more space by getting rid of a few large items than by removing a lot of smaller ones. Consider whether you really need all your furniture. Does it actually get used? Or is it just taking up room that could be used more effectively or left empty to create a greater sense of space?

Now, what are you going to do with all these things you're clearing out? Here are some possibilities:

- Give things to friends.
- Donate good-quality items to a local thrift shop.
- Used bookstores will probably buy boxes of books from you.
- Take the rest to the dump or rent a small dumpster for a few days if you have a lot to throw out.

Storing what you have more efficiently

Even when you have thrown out everything you can, the house may still feel cluttered. If it irritates you now, that's nothing compared with how you'll feel when you have sleepless nights and all the chores involved with having a small baby.

The way to unclutter your house, once you've gotten rid of everything you can, is to store the rest of it more effectively. The most important principle to follow here is that the neater things are, the more efficiently you can store them. Underwear thrown into a drawer occupies more space than it would if it were neatly stacked. Not all of us can bring ourselves to fold our underwear carefully every time we wash it, but even smoothing it vaguely flat will make it easier to store.

The idea of storing things neatly applies to all clothes and also to the contents of your bathroom and kitchen cabinets, home office, shed, and everything else. The coffee table in the living room will look a hundred times better if you simply straighten up the piles of books and magazines. And a neater, less cluttered look will help you feel more relaxed.

To store everything efficiently, you also need to keep things in appropriate-sized storage spaces. If you allow yourself four drawers for household paperwork, you can bet it will fill four drawers. But efficient and tidy storage (getting rid of everything you don't need) might enable you to fit it into only two drawers—leaving two free for something else. It is equally inefficient to cram all your tableware into one small cabinet so that in order to get any item out you have to take out three other things first.

Matching the storage space to the amount you need to store in it might mean swapping the contents of some cupboards or shelves for others. For example, moving the spare towels from the linen cupboard to a towel storage rack in the bathroom could release valuable storage space within reach of all the bedrooms.

To keep your home neat, get into the habit of putting things away every time you use them. You'll soon do it without thinking, and you'll never need to spend more than a moment or two straightening up.

Pretty hanging storage can be used for small items such as soft toys.

Clearing the kitchen

Baby in the kitchen

There are quite a few extra things that will be kept in the kitchen when the baby arrives, so you need to allocate space for them all. Baby items in the kitchen include:

- Sterilizer
- Bottles
- Bowls, spoons, cups, etc.
- Bibs
- Baby food
- Baby-food processor
- High chair

Simply keeping your kitchen clear and clean gives you more space to operate in.

The more space you can clear in the kitchen, the better—you can't have too much, as your baby is going to fill all the space you can clear. Since the kitchen is a room where you are often busy, rather than one where you simply relax, it's doubly important to keep it clean and clutter-free.

Most of the suggestions here are easy to put into practice. A few of them might entail investing in new furniture or furnishings, but you don't have to do this all at once, especially while you're saving for the expense of a new member of the family. Plan what you would like to change, and do it as you can afford it. Aim to change the things that will make the biggest difference first.

A streamlined space

For a start, you can go through your food cupboards and get rid of anything that is past its expiration date. And throw out or give away anything you'll never use, such as that can of luxury pâté you were given for Christmas but don't actually like.

Be ruthless about getting rid of serving bowls, pitchers, and other pieces of tableware that you never use. Be especially brutal about gadgets you hardly use, from egg-slicers to frosting bags. Try to keep your kitchen equipment as near as possible to the place you need it; it makes for a much easier life. For example, keep your wooden spoons and spatulas in a pot next to the stove rather than in a drawer on the other side of the room.

Furniture can also be a big cause of clutter in the kitchen. Make sure you have chairs that can be pushed right in under the table. If your kitchen storage is freestanding, aim to have one or two big pieces of furniture rather than several smaller ones. The more everything matches, the less cluttered it will look and feel. This doesn't mean you have to avoid having separate pieces, but you can make them look more uniform. The simplest way is to paint most or all of your furniture in the same color range. If it's unpainted, your furniture will look more harmonious and calm if it's all the same color of wood rather than a mixture of, say, oak and pine.

Clear a shelf or a cupboard in the kitchen for keeping all the food and basic equipment you need for your baby, from jars to bibs, bowls, and spoons.

Kitchen tips

- Open shelves can help a small kitchen appear bigger than cabinets do, maximizing the sense of space. (However, they are most suitable for items you use a lot, which won't collect dust.)
- A narrow shelf a little above the kitchen work surface will hold everything you normally keep *on* the work surface, leaving it clear for food preparation instead.
- If your shelves are significantly higher than the jars and packages you keep on them, add another shelf a little above the other ones. Finding everything will still be easy, even if this new shelf is narrower than the existing ones.
- If you have any wall space in your kitchen, use it for storage. Put up a plate rack, hang up your pans near the stovetop, or put all your mugs on a row of hooks.
- Blinds or shades rather than curtains at the window will give much more of a feeling of space, as well as being more practical.

If you do choose open shelving, however, be aware of safety. Ensure that babies or young children cannot reach any potentially dangerous items such as heavy or sharp cooking utensils, crockery, glassware, and cleaning fluids.

Clearing the bathroom

Bathroom tips

- If you have a small bathroom, find furniture that doubles as storage, such as a stool with a seat that lifts up to reveal a storage box underneath.
- If your laundry basket has to be in the bathroom, at least get one you can sit on.
- Once your baby is mobile, you'll need a lockable medicine cabinet, out of reach, for storing anything from medicines to razor blades.
- Find somewhere to hang towels that doesn't take up wall space, such as in front of a radiator or on rails below the sink. This can leave a large area of wall free to put furniture against.
- Once your child is big enough to use the bathtub, you'll probably want room for a chair or stool for you to sit on while he is bathing.
- Don't waste the space under the sink. If you aren't hanging towels beneath it, box it in to make a vanity unit.
- Glass shelves in front of the window provide useful storage and look attractive with glass bottles and bath oils on them. (Make sure small children can't reach them, for safety reasons.)

Bathrooms are often small, despite being one of the most functional rooms in the house and one of the busiest at certain times of day. Efficient storage is essential here.

It may be possible to move certain items out of the bathroom altogether, which will release valuable space. For example, all toiletries that are not used on a daily basis, as well as cleaning materials and toilet paper, could be stored outside the bathroom, perhaps in a bedroom, on the landing, or in a hall closet.

Bathrooms are especially prone to feeling cluttered simply because of the way they are decorated and furnished. Because they are usually small and full of functional things, a simple, streamlined feel is, in fact, all the more important. What's more, the bathroom is often the

parents' sanctuary and so it needs to be as relaxing and refreshing as possible.

The chief culprits for making bathrooms feel cramped and messy are curtains—window curtains and shower curtains. Keep these simple, choosing pale colors without ruffles or busy patterns. A blind or shade at the window is often better than a curtain and can sit inside the window frame. If the windowsill is an important storage area that you really can't give up, stick to curtains but keep them light and simple.

Follow the same guidelines for decorating the bathroom as a whole. Light, bright colors, clean lines, and no fussy frills and patterns will help you create a room that feels spacious and uncluttered, which you can enjoy spending time in.

Baby in the bathroom

Some of the things that may need space in your bathroom when the baby arrives are:

- Baby bath
- Baby towels
- Diapers
- Absorbent cotton and baby wipes
- Talcum powder, baby bath oil, soap, baby shampoo, and other toiletries

A spacious laundry basket will discourage the family from leaving dirty clothes on the bathroom floor.

Clearing the rest of the house

Little and often

To keep rooms neat, the advice is simple—straighten up frequently, as often as several times a day, and it will take so little time you won't even notice you're doing it. If you allow everything to build up, clearing it away becomes a mammoth task.

Once you get into the habit of frequent straightening up, it becomes easy. If it's not your usual style, make yourself do it for just a couple of weeks and soon it will be automatic.

Once you get into the habit of being neat, you'll really appreciate being able to find things easily.

Although the kitchen and the bathroom are arguably the busiest rooms in the house and consequently very prone to clutter, you will probably need to clear all the other rooms, too. An efficiently cleared house will help you to feel calmer and less frazzled and will be easier to function in.

Entrance hall

The entrance hall is all too easy to fill. Things get dumped there as everyone comes in and often don't get put away properly. If you already have other children, this will be especially true. The answer is twofold:
• Provide storage for everything that needs to be kept in the entrance hall.
• Be thorough about moving everything else to the place where it should be kept.

You are bound to need hooks for coats, either in a coat closet or on the wall. You will possibly also want a place for boots, outdoor shoes, bags, and briefcases, and a shelf or table for keeping keys, loose change, and other small items. Depending on the other space you have in the house, you may end up storing a stroller and perhaps the baby's car seat in the entrance hall, too.

If space is at a premium, choose furniture that is space-efficient. A narrow cupboard, for example, can be dual-purpose; letters that are to be mailed can be kept on top, and boots inside. And don't waste the walls—a key cupboard and eye-level shelves above other furniture help to maximize space.

Living room

This is your main area for relaxing and putting your feet up, so it's important to keep this room feeling calm and spacious. If it seems cluttered, consider whether you could rearrange the furniture.

You can also remove a few pillows, or change upholstery and curtain fabrics from busy patterns to simpler ones, to give a more open effect. Neatening the contents of shelves is a big help, too. If your bookshelves are filled with junk or the books are piled on top of each other, straightening up will make a difference.

You may be keeping all sorts of toys in here, so try to allocate some space for them, preferably a cupboard or somewhere you can hide the toys away in the evenings. If you don't create this extra space now, you'll simply find the room cluttered again in a few months.

Master bedroom

If the baby is going to sleep in his own room, he shouldn't impinge too much on your bedroom. If the baby is going to sleep with you, however, you may need to find room for a cradle or a crib and a changing station for nighttime diaper changes. This might also be the room where you plan to keep the baby's clothes, in which case you will need storage for them, too. Bedrooms often have little space for extra furniture, so you may find that your best option is to ruthlessly clear out the drawers and closets you already have.

Utility room

Don't forget this room, which is purely functional and therefore an important place to keep uncluttered. You're going to have a lot more laundry to deal with when the baby arrives, and you may also want to use this room for storing baby things, like a diaper pail and some of the items you would otherwise keep in the kitchen such as a sterilizer and, later on, a high chair.

You'll need plenty of storage units or chests to house all the baby's toys.

Clearing other spaces

Driving with your baby
You may keep a lot of baby things in your car, including:
- Car seat
- Diaper bag
- Stroller
- Sunshade, rain cover, and cozy cover for the stroller
- Sunshade for the car window
- Baby toys for the car

The house probably seems like the obvious area to clean and clear, but it's not the only one. The garage, the yard, and even the car will all benefit from the same exercise. When your baby is still small, it feels wrong to take him into a space that is messy or dirty, and that includes any areas outside the house where you're likely to spend time with him.

The backyard
You may not take your new baby out into the yard much in the winter months, but in the summer there are few more pleasant places to spend time with him. It is much more natural for your child to hear the birds singing and feel the breeze against his skin than to stay indoors listening to the buzz of the refrigerator or the ringing of the phone.

Tidy the yard before the baby arrives. Throw out any old or broken garden furniture and equipment, and trim overgrown flower beds. If you know you're not going to be able to maintain the beds in good condition, consider replacing them with lawn, paving, or something else attractive and more manageable. You'll need shady areas for your baby, but ensure there are no poisonous plants within reach.

The garage and other outbuildings
If you keep your car in the garage or have any other buildings where you and your baby are likely to spend any time, clean them in preparation for the baby's arrival. It's a therapeutic exercise, and it creates a cleaner and calmer environment for your baby.

As usual, clear out anything unwanted or broken, and store the rest efficiently. Take safety into account, too; it won't be long until your child is able to reach tools, the lawnmower, and other dangerous equipment. Even at three months, a baby can put a hand out and touch anything within reach as you carry him past.

The car
This is an extension of your house and one in which your baby will spend a lot of time. Clean your car thoroughly inside and make sure it is in a state that you'd like a tiny baby to travel in. If your baby is born in a hospital, he will encounter the car even before your home.

Remember that any unanchored, heavy objects in the car will be a danger to both you and your baby in an accident. So don't keep loose gasoline cans, tool kits, or anything else in the passenger compartment.

Your baby will enjoy sleeping outdoors in a safe, quiet, and shady spot.

Cleansing

Open the windows wide and let the fresh air into the house after you've spring-cleaned.

Once you've finished clearing your house, garage, and car, it's time for a thorough clean. Because babies are susceptible to many germs and impurities, they need a clean environment. But it's more than that—if a place is to become a sanctuary for your baby, it needs to go through a deep cleansing.

Begin by spring-cleaning the whole house so that it feels fresh and clean. Then air the house thoroughly, opening the windows and letting the fresh air stream in, to reach every corner. Once you've gone through this process, keep the house clean until the birth (and after it). If you're lucky, you may well get a sudden urge to clean the place again a few weeks or days before the baby is born; many women "nest" in this way.

Enlist the cooperation of the rest of the household, too. When you're heavily pregnant is no time to launch into industrial-level cleaning every few days. Encourage everyone in your family to respect this newly clean environment and to keep it that way. If everyone clears up after themselves, the job of cleaning is far less onerous.

Cleansing rituals

Smudging is a Native American tradition that is becoming increasingly popular. A method of ritual cleansing, it aims to remove any negative energies from the home and can be used to cleanse it in readiness for the arrival of your baby. It entails purifying the house by carrying incense around it so that the smoke from it permeates the whole building.

You can buy incense specially made for the purpose, in bundles of sticks or as powder, which you can carry in a bowl or a shell. Or you can simply buy any incense sticks or use the natural plants to achieve the same effect. The traditional plants used for smudging are sage (the most commonly used plant), cedar, or sweet grass. You can also use other cleansing herbs like juniper or mint.

Smudging

1 To perform the smudging ritual, stand in the east side of the house. Light the incense or smudging sticks, and begin by smudging yourself, holding the incense above your head and then moving it down to the floor while oscillating it in front of you.

2 Repeat this on your right side, from your head down to the floor, then at your back, and then on your left side.

3 Next, describe a circle clockwise above your head three times with the incense.

4 Finally, starting in the east of the house, walk clockwise around it from room to room, visualizing the smoke cleansing the house as you go. Linger a little in the places that will be especially important to the baby, such as above its crib.

Repeat this ritual as often as you like until the baby is born. You can continue after the birth, too, but don't expose your baby directly to the smoke.

3
Creating
a place of
harmony and
tranquility

Using feng shui

Feng shui (pronounced "fung shway") is the ancient Chinese art of arranging your surroundings to maximize the beneficial flow of universal energy, known as chi or qi (pronounced "chee"). This energy exists in and around everything. The idea is that chi should keep moving all the time in order to bring good feng shui. Correct feng shui gives a place an instinctively calm and harmonious atmosphere, which is exactly what your baby needs in order to enjoy a peaceful first few months and beyond.

Chi needs to be calm and tranquil in order to be harmonious, but it shouldn't stop flowing altogether or it stagnates and the energy, or atmosphere, of the place becomes dead and stultifying. The aim is to encourage the chi to flow at a steady, balanced rate, like a gentle stream. There can be little eddies and currents, but no rapids and no stagnant areas.

A natural balance

In order to achieve the right flow of chi, you need to know what it likes. Chi will move at a pleasant, gentle rate when it has plenty of light and air—it likes open spaces and gentle curves to flow around. It enters a room through the doors and windows, and will move freely around a space with good feng shui, getting into all the corners. It doesn't easily flow into dark corners, nooks, and crannies, so these need to be eliminated or at least should be adapted (as we'll see) to encourage the chi to enter them.

You can think of the process of encouraging chi as being akin to airing the home. You want the fresh air to get into all the corners, but you don't want drafts, let alone a gale, blowing through the house.

Speeding up the flow

If you have dark cubbyholes and corners, small rooms, or cluttered areas in your house, the chi will be unable to flow smoothly and bring harmony to the room. Clearing them out is therefore the first step in removing obstacles that would interrupt the chi's flow. After that, you can improve matters

Improve the chi of a room by bringing in light and movement. A colorful mobile over the baby's cradle or crib energizes chi in the nursery (see opposite).

using one of the following traditional feng shui remedies, which will energize chi that is stagnating in such places:

LIGHT: Let more light in through a window, perhaps by opening the curtains further. Consider using stronger lightbulbs, adding a light in a dark corner, or adding mirrors to a room to reflect and multiply incoming light.

SOUND: Wind chimes are the classic feng shui remedy here, but you could use anything from an indoor water feature to a CD/DVD player.

MOVEMENT: Anything that moves works to liven up chi in dead areas, including a flag, a water feature, wind chimes (again), or the smoke from incense (but don't expose babies directly to smoke). The obvious movement remedy around babies is a mobile.

MECHANICAL DEVICES: These are items that are functional and move or run on electricity, such as a television or an electric fan. If too much electricity gives the air an unpleasant buzz, use an electric clock instead. In a baby's nursery you might use a revolving night-light (see page 48).

Nursery tips

- Make sure there's plenty of light in the room. If there are any dark corners, use a remedy to lighten them (see page 49).
- Give your baby a cradle or crib that is up off the floor so that chi can flow under and around it.
- Position the cradle or crib away from any windows and in a place from which the door is visible (in other words, not right behind the door or behind a bookshelf or other form of screen).
- Don't put the cradle or crib immediately under a light fixture.

Plants add life to your home, both literally and metaphorically.

COLOR: This remedy is especially associated with children, so it's an ideal one to choose for rooms your baby will spend time in. Light or bright colors will help keep chi moving. Even if you like to decorate in pale tones, a splash of bright color can enliven a room.

LIFE: The obvious example here is plants, which encourage chi to visit the corners and shelves on which you place them. Any living plant will bring good feng shui to these areas, but you should, of course, avoid poisonous plants around babies and small children. An alternative example is fish in a tank.

Slowing down the flow

Sometimes chi moves too fast, for example in long hallways and corridors, or down straight staircases. Outdoors, straight garden paths often speed the flow of chi away from the home. You can generally sense these places because they are not areas of the home where you want to linger; they have a restless feel about them. Broadly speaking, chi doesn't like straight lines because of this tendency for it to rush through too fast. Two feng shui remedies are therefore used to slow down, rather than speed up, chi:

STILLNESS: A statue or other large, heavy object will cause the chi to slow down. In a long straight hall or corridor, a single attractive object will soothe the restless atmosphere.

STRAIGHT LINES: You can break up chi that is directed straight down a corridor or path by positioning a straight object such as a stick of bamboo in such a way as to reroute the chi at an angle of about forty-five degrees to the corridor. Hanging a wallpaper with vertical lines or checks can also fulfill this function.

Feng shui in the nursery

In addition to the basic principles of feng shui, there are specific guidelines for keeping the chi flowing smoothly in different parts of the home. The most obvious room to tackle first is your new baby's nursery.

If you have a choice about which room to use as a nursery, choose one in a position that feels safe. This may well mean a room at the back of the house and close to your own. A cozy (but not too tiny) room is preferable to one that is very large with high ceilings (there's a lot of plain common sense in feng shui). If possible, a room in the north or east of the house is the perfect spot for a baby.

Feng shui in the kitchen

Kitchens can be very busy, cluttered rooms if you're not careful. Since you spend a lot of time in here, it's inevitable that your baby will, too. Keep the room as calm and tranquil as you can to preserve the harmonious feng shui.

• Make sure the room is light and bright, with no dark corners. You can't have too much lighting in a kitchen. Add mirrors or mirror tiles or use chrome equipment to make the most of the room's natural light.

• Work hard to keep the room neat, and make sure there's enough storage to make this possible. Allow yourself plenty of free work surfaces.

• Keep electrical equipment in good working order (it's bad feng shui to leave an item broken).

• Counteract all that electricity by keeping plants in your kitchen—herbs are an obvious choice. Fresh flowers on the table also give a splash of color and freshness.

Feng shui in the bathroom

The bathroom should be a place of relaxation and pleasure for both you and your baby. Bathtime is a wonderful way to unwind before bed, and good feng shui will help. Water is a natural element of feng shui (the term literally means "wind and water"), so your bathroom already contains plenty of remedies—movement, sound, mechanical devices (faucets), and reflected light.

• Keep the bathroom uncluttered; there should be as much room as possible to move around freely.

• The movement, light, and sound of the water will keep the chi moving. Use soothing colors to keep it from becoming too vibrant.

• Make sure you can see the door from the bathtub and from the baby's bath. If it's around a corner, place a mirror so you can see the door.

Feng shui in the living room

This may double as your child's playroom. It is very easy for the room to become cluttered and messy, which will mean the chi tends to stagnate. Counteract this tendency with the following remedies:

• Provide plenty of storage so that your baby's toys can be put away when they're not being used.

• Make sure the room is cozy and friendly but don't fill it with ornaments.

• Think carefully about where to place the main furniture and seating so it doesn't form an obstacle course.

Wind chimes are an ideal way to introduce both sound and movement in the garden or near an open window.

Making the nursery safe

Over the first few months, your child's safety needs will change. The more she is able to reach out and grab things or to roll over, the more precautions you'll need to take. The following safety features are worth designing into the nursery from the start:

- Keep all changing equipment, such as diapers, cotton, and talcum powder, within reach of the changing table but out of the baby's reach.
- Keep any medicines well out of reach.
- On the changing table, use a changing mat that has a raised portion all around the edge to help prevent the baby from rolling off it.
- Avoid toy chests with lift-up lids, which can come down on a child's head.
- Make air holes inside any chests or cupboards.
- Attach to the wall any furniture that could topple over.
- Put safety catches on drawers to keep a small child from opening them and pulling them—or the whole chest—down on herself.

Give yourself plenty of time to buy suitable toys and prepare the nursery before your baby's arrival.

Preparing the nursery

By the time you're about seven months pregnant, you'll want to start getting the nursery ready. If your baby has her own nursery, she will sleep in there every night and probably take naps there, too. It may also be the place where you feed her during the day and at night, change diapers, and spend time just playing with your baby. In other words, the room may need to fulfill many and various functions.

However, this is fundamentally a room for sleeping in, and so it's a good idea to decorate it in restful tones. Save the primary colors for the playroom. You'll obviously want the room to look warm and inviting from the start, but it's essential not to overcrowd it at this stage—it will start filling up with toys, pictures, small furniture, and so on within a few months.

When you set out to prepare the nursery, you'll find no shortage of things to fit into it:
- Crib and/or cradle
- Chair
- Changing table
- Toy storage
- Clothes storage
- Lighting
- Baby monitor
- Shelves
- First toys/mobiles

The most important piece of furniture for the first few months will be the crib. It's the one place where you'll leave your baby unattended, so it needs to be safe. It's your baby's ultimate sanctuary after it leaves the womb. Make sure that whatever crib you use meets all safety standards. It's important that the slats or bars are close enough together— they must be no more than 2.5 in. apart—and that the mattress fits snugly, with no dangerous gaps around the edges.

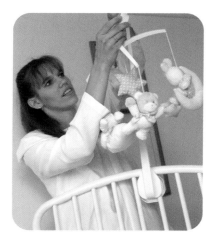

The position of the crib is important, too. It must be away from windows and from anything dangerous that the baby could reach once she starts to sit or stand, such as heaters, lights, cords, small toys she could swallow, stickers, decorations, and furniture she could

A night-light will enable you to check on your baby without disturbing her.

use to help climb out of the crib.

Once the crib is safe, you can think about making it welcoming. Positioning it against a wall and using bumper pads (until your child is old enough to climb on them) give it a feeling of security and helps prevent drafts. Add mobiles and other hanging toys that meet current safety standards, but bear in mind that you'll have to remove them once your baby can reach them.

If your baby is going to sleep in a Moses basket or bassinet for the first few months, you can put this in the crib at nighttime. When she outgrows the basket, it will be easy to remove it and put her straight into the crib; she may hardly notice the change.

Creating a nursing corner

If you're going to breast-feed your baby in the nursery, you'll be spending a lot of time in there and you'll want to create your own personal nursing sanctuary. Even if you only give nighttime feedings in the nursery, you will still be there for quite a while. Each feed could take about an hour when your baby is tiny, and some babies feed for longer. You therefore need to be comfortable and occupied.

The ideal solution is to create a corner where you have everything you need to nurse your baby, so you can thoroughly enjoy the experience. Here are some suggestions:

• Comfort is the first essential. Choose a chair for nursing that supports your back, neck, and shoulders and has either low armrests or none at all.

• You may want to put your feet up, and a footstool or low table is ideal. Or you could opt for a chair with short legs or get a recliner.

• Due to some design flaw of nature, a small baby cannot rest on your lap and reach your breast; you'll need to rest her on pillows to bring her up to the right height. Many mothers find a large, long beanbag very comfortable to take the baby's weight, and there are some that are designed especially for feeding.

• Have a quilt or blanket nearby to keep you warm when you're feeding at night, and, of course, a blanket for the baby to snuggle into.

• You'll need a table within reach to keep things on while you're feeding, particularly a drink and some snacks, such as fruit or crackers, to replace the energy your body uses breast-feeding.

• Keep something handy to occupy you while you breast-feed, such as books or magazines.

• A radio or cassette/CD player is also useful when you're breast-feeding. Again, keep this (or a remote control for it) on the table beside your nursing chair.

Try creating a haven like this, you'll find nursing your baby a thoroughly enjoyable experience and excellent time out from the busy life you'll be leading.

You can put a night-light on the crib or right next to it—some are available that project lights onto the walls and ceiling. Obviously it should conform to safety standards and will need to be removed before your baby is able to reach it.

Lighting the nursery

There are times when you need plenty of light in the nursery, such as for changing diapers or playing, and there are times when the baby is asleep when you want dim lighting. The lighting will therefore need to be flexible. Small babies are not afraid of the dark (they've just spent nine months without light in the womb), but you can't check on your baby unless there is some light in the room. Turning lights on and off may disturb her, so you may prefer to have permanent low light at night (though as she gets older, she may come to depend on the light and dislike the dark). Here are some ideas for lighting the nursery:

• A dimmer switch on the main light is useful.

• Heavy curtains, or curtains with a blackout lining, that cut out most of the light outside will enable you to darken the room during the day. They will also be very welcome in the summer months when children may otherwise awaken early as it becomes light outside.

• A sidelight can be useful, especially at bedtime. Make sure your baby can't reach the light, the cord, or the outlet.

• Consider using a night-light that plugs directly into an outlet. It will give a low light, but it will be just enough to check on your baby at night.

Eliminating the unwanted

Getting the house into shape

Once your baby is born, you will probably have very little time for anything that isn't essential. Feeding takes up a lot of time with some babies, and you may feel very tired for a few months. This is why the last few months of pregnancy are a good time to get the house into shape so that it runs smoothly when the baby arrives. That is the time to fix those leaky faucets, replace the washing machine, mend rickety shelves, fix the squeaky stairs, repair the lock on the back door, and do all those other little jobs that will help make the house tranquil and restful—and which you may not get another chance to do for some months.

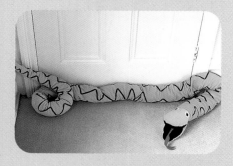

Keep your baby's nursery cozy and free from drafts.

As well as acquiring everything you're going to need for your new baby, you should also get rid of everything you don't want. We've looked at uncluttering the house in Chapter 2, but there are other things to deal with.

Extremes of temperature

Babies can't regulate their own temperature, so you have to do it for them. While you can add or remove clothes and blankets, it helps if your home is a stable temperature. If it is to feel like a sanctuary for your baby, it must be comfortable.

Make sure that any room your child is going to spend time in can easily be kept at a pleasant temperature. If the room is cold, invest in a heater of some kind, and eliminate any drafts with draft excluders at the bottom of the door and around the windows.

As explained on page 12, overheating is at least as bad for your baby as being in a draft. So if you have rooms that tend to get very hot in the summer, you could replace windows that don't open with ones that do, or install an overhead fan. If you have a large range that makes the kitchen too hot in the summer, you might consider buying a small, countertop oven to use instead.

Insect invaders

Few everyday irritations can be as frustrating to babies as insect bites, especially when they are too small to be able to scratch. Protect your baby from insects, especially at night. Use screens on the windows, and hang a mosquito net around the crib.

Keeping the noise down

It's unnecessary to bring your child up in near silence or refuse to allow any sound when the baby is asleep. Babies with older siblings will sleep right through their commotion and even a first child is often oblivious to an astonishing amount of background noise.

However, too much noise is stressful for everyone, and your stress will be detrimental to the baby. So if your house is prone to any irritating noises, get them fixed or at least minimized. Repair banging pipes or consider double glazing to reduce outside noise. If this is too expensive, perhaps you could install it just in the baby's bedroom.

If you have noisy older children and you want to reduce the noise, introduce new systems before the baby is born. You might insist that the door stays closed when the television is on or that a maximum volume is set on their music.

Your baby will thrive in a peaceful nursery. If insects are a particular problem, protect her by using a mosquito net over the crib at night.

Natural diapers

There are lots of options for your baby's diapers, but the key choice is between disposable and cloth. There is no organic disposable diaper on the market that is totally environmentally friendly. However, some brands of disposables aim to be as natural as possible and better for your baby and the environment than others.

- Not all reusable diapers are organic, but many are. They are generally better for the environment than disposables and work out to be cheaper over time, although the initial investment is high. However, they do not suit all babies. Not only do they tend to be bulkier than disposables, but they can make some babies with sensitive skin more prone to diaper rash.
- If you're unsure which option to go for, ask friends with children which choice they made and why. You should be able to find a salesperson who can discuss several brands of reusable diapers with you, and advise you on which are organic. Look for ads in baby magazines or local papers, or ask your doctor or hospital if they can direct you to a local retailer.

A wide range of organic baby foods are available in most supermarkets.

Going organic

There is much debate nowadays about whether or not pesticides, food additives, and other chemicals are harmful. Some clearly are, while others are still unknown quantities. It may do your baby no harm at all to eat treated or genetically modified foods and to use nonorganic materials. Then again, some of them may damage your baby's delicate system.

The safest bet is to go organic. Organic products aren't cheap, of course, but you don't have to use them exclusively. There's a vast range of organic options available, including:

- Baby food
- Fresh fruit and vegetables
- Diapers
- Clothing
- Bedding
- Baby carriers

Jars of organic baby food are readily available in supermarkets, and you can also buy fresh organic foods to feed your baby. Uncooked bananas and avocados are suitable as soon as your baby is on solid food, and you can stew and puree a wide range of other fruits and vegetables, such as apples, pears, squash, and carrots.

If you have the time and the space, the best way to bring your baby up on organic food is to grow it yourself. That way, you know exactly what you're feeding them. Even if you have only a tiny vegetable patch or just a couple of apple trees, it all contributes to a healthy start for your baby.

Natural foods

You can start feeding your baby pureed fresh fruits and vegetables when she is between four and six months old. At this early age it is reassuring to know your baby's food is pure and organic.

Relationships in the family

The single biggest factor in determining how harmonious a home your baby will be born into must be the family itself. You and your partner, along with any other children, have the power to create a sanctuary for your new baby just by your behavior, even if you live in a tiny apartment or share a home with other family members such as parents.

Babies are highly sensitive to the atmosphere around them, so it is important to make sure they are surrounded by harmony and happiness, rather than stress and discord. Even if you have other children, you and your partner are the biggest influence on this. Agree before the birth that you will aim to keep a happy and relaxed mood around the baby at all times.

It's not always easy to stay cheerful, especially when you are still learning to cope with a new baby. And some couples naturally argue as their way of resolving problems. But realistically you can still agree on two things:

• If tension builds up, you will talk about it as soon as you recognize it, rather than waiting until one or both of you reach the boiling point.

• If you find yourselves raising your voices and getting angry, you will move out of the baby's earshot.

Make it easy for yourselves
Tensions often arise after the birth of a new baby. Happy as the event is, there's no denying that it can leave you exhausted and can be the start of weeks of broken nights. If this is your first child, there's also the stress of coping with the new responsibility. If you already have children, they can go through a tricky period when the birth of a baby brother or sister places more demands on you. The following tips may help keep your relationship on the rails:

• Set aside time together as often as you can. Evenings are good for this; even if you're quietly nursing the baby at the same time, you can still talk. There are always chores to be done, but leave them for half an hour or so—this is more important.

• Keep checking how your partner is coping; don't assume he is on top of it all. Just because it's tough for you, doesn't mean it isn't tough for him, too.

• Sleep in separate beds from time to time if it means one of you can catch up on sleep, but don't let it turn into a habit.

• Make sure you both feel the other is pulling their weight; it's easy for resentments to grow. One of the simplest approaches is to agree that neither of you stops to rest at the end of the day until everything is done. Even if your partner is out at work all day, he pitches in when he gets home until you can both stop and sit down. (If he thinks going out to work all day is tougher, get him to spend all day with the baby on the weekend. That should persuade him that you need to rest at the end of the day as much as he does.)

• Take turns looking after the baby, getting up at night, and dealing with the other children. Apart from breast-feeding, there's nothing that can't be done equally well by either partner, and sharing in this way helps you feel more like a unified team. It's an important boost to your relationship.

Getting siblings on board

As explained on page 22, it's essential to prepare older siblings for what to expect, so there aren't too many surprises when the new baby arrives. Then get them

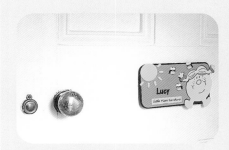

Make sure that your older children have opportunities for privacy away from the baby.

Babies usually revel in attention from their older siblings.

Toilet humor
Preschool children not only are fascinated by bodily functions, but consider themselves experts on anything to do with pee and poo. You can get a small child interested in the new baby simply by discussing the finer points of diapers and their contents.

on board by enlisting their support. If you tell them how valuable they'll be, and how much their little brother or sister will learn from them and love them, you will instill a sense of pride and responsibility.

Once the baby arrives, continue this approach by encouraging your child to help you look after her. Don't apply any pressure, but many children will want to join in. They can, for example, pass you the wipes at changing time or fetch the bib from the drawer.

Fitting in with the new routines
If you have an older child or children, they may well adapt to the baby's arrival more easily than a young child, so long as you can be flexible about fitting the baby's needs around them. If you tell them that soccer practice is canceled for the next few months because it will clash with feeding time, you could be in for trouble, but some careful scheduling should prevent most problems.

No matter how you try to minimize the disruption to your children's lifestyle, some change will be unavoidable after the baby arrives. For a start, you will be less available. And you may need them to keep the noise down or fit activities around the baby's feedings or nap times.

Clearly, the more you can avoid changing your children's routines, the better. But when it is unavoidable, try following these suggestions:
• Give them as much warning as possible.
• Explain the reason why it is necessary for them to adapt.
• Acknowledge that it's not ideal, but point out the benefits or offer compensations ("I can't play that with you at the moment, but I'll read you a story instead.").
• Don't keep telling them they can't have what they want "because of the baby," otherwise jealousies are bound to build up.
• Let them know how grown up they're being and appeal to their burgeoning sense of independence. You can start letting them do some things for themselves, such as pouring their own drinks, which makes them feel grown-up and saves you the effort. If they're older, perhaps now is the time to let them cycle to their friend's house on their own instead of getting a ride from you. The more self-reliant they are, the less jealous they are likely to feel of the baby's helplessness.
• Always remember to praise them for being cooperative.

Make sure you spend some relaxing time together as a family and do your best to help older children accept the baby.

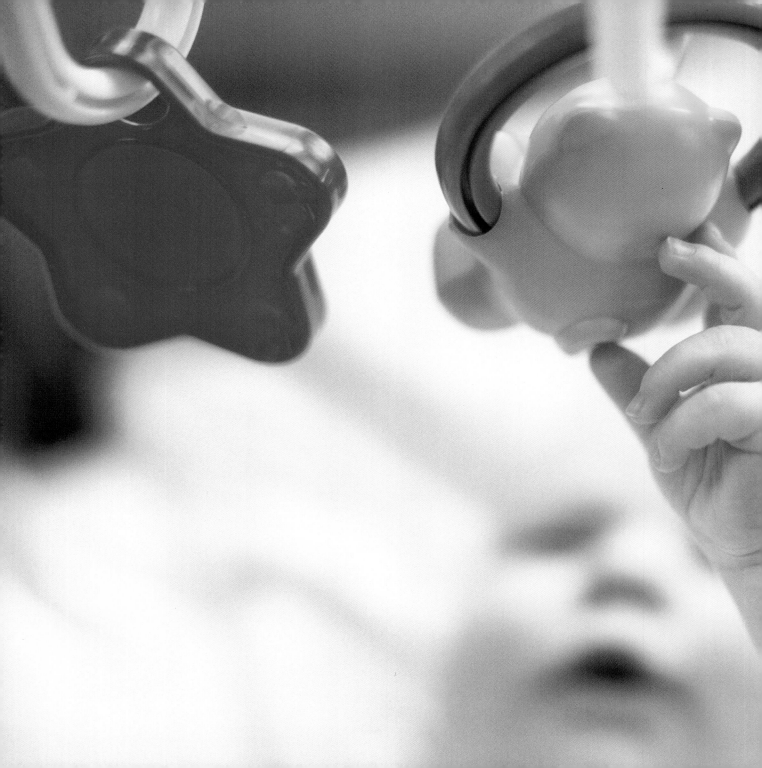

4

Introducing color, light, movement, and sound

The psychology of color

Colors have a deep impact on our psyches; why else would we talk about "black moods," "feeling blue," "seeing red," or having a "sunny disposition"? Babies are as susceptible as anyone else to this, so you'll need to give some thought to the colors you surround your new baby with.

Because different colors will generate different responses, the colors should be chosen to suit the room in question. Choose restful shades for the bedroom to encourage your baby to sleep, while more stimulating colors will suit the parts of your house where the baby will be awake and playing. If you're planning a nursery where your child will both play and sleep, a combination of peaceful and energizing colors is the ideal solution.

Stimulating colors

The exciting, hot colors that will stimulate your child's mind are reds, oranges, and yellows. All of these hues come in different shades, and the brighter and stronger they are, the more they will stimulate your child. For example, sunflower yellow is more vibrant and revitalizing than primrose yellow.

It is possible to overstimulate your child, which can cause frustration and fractiousness. Therefore, avoid blasting a room with very hot colors. Use some softer shades, such as apricot instead of orange, to tone down the overall effect.

Soothing and relaxing colors

The colors that will help to calm your child are greens, blues, and gentle violets. The paler these tones, the more relaxing they are.

A scheme of only pale colors, however, can look too bland. To avoid this, add splashes of stimulating colors like bright peacock blues and emerald greens, which will add vibrant accents without making the overall effect too exciting.

Neutrals such as creams are relaxing, but these, too, can benefit from a spark of stronger color to liven them up. White is very cold and it is generally better to soothe your baby with warmer, off-white shades.

Choose soothing colors, such as soft blue, green, and lemon, for the baby's blankets and crib bumpers.

Use borders and curtains to bring splashes of color to the nursery.

Suiting your own style

Suppose you personally like restful pastel shades; do you have to decorate your living room in primary colors to stimulate your baby at playtime? Of course not. Your living room is there for you to relax in, as much as for your baby to play in. The answer is to use your favorite relaxing colors, but to include accents in stronger hues. For example, decorate in neutral shades, but add flashes of color in fabrics and accessories.

Decorating with color

Paint and wallpaper are the most obvious means of bringing color into your baby's nursery or playroom. But while the walls often set the dominant theme for a room, there are plenty of other ways of injecting color into your decorating scheme, especially through the use of fabric.

It's a good idea to use the main color on the walls, in either paint or wallpaper, and then to temper the effect with bedding, curtains, and other fabrics. You might want to choose hot reds and pinks for the playroom walls, but tone them down with soft pink and creamy curtains and chair covers.

Alternatively, the bedroom walls could be soft pastel blue but the bedding bright red and white. This variety is more interesting for your baby than picking a medium shade and using it for everything in the room.

Bright wallpapers and borders are a simple and effective way to bring color into a room.

Lighting

The light that you bring into a room—both natural and artificial—will have a strong impact on the overall color scheme. Sunny colors look great in a sunny room, but can look muddy in a dimly lit room. These darker rooms often look best when decorated in cozy, warm colors.

Hot colors work much better when there is plenty of light for them to reflect back, so if you want to use oranges and reds, make sure the room has enough light. If natural light is scarce, use lots of artificial light.

You can also add color with tinted bulbs and lights. Warm tints will offset the starkness of a very pale or white room and will make strong colors feel even cozier. This can be a particular advantage in creating a snug, womblike bedroom for your baby.

Using paint

The obvious place to put paint is on the walls, but you can bring a lot of warmth and color to a room by painting the window frames, closet doors, and furniture. Have fun expressing your creativity by personalizing your baby's new room in your own way. This can turn off-the-rack wallpaper and

You'll find a huge range of colorful lights available for nurseries.

furnishings into something really special for your child.

Why not paint his name in bright colors on a chair or chest of drawers, or even paint the whole piece of furniture? If you feel artistically inclined, you can paint murals or your own frieze on the walls. If you're not confident of your skills, paint simple colored stripes or geometric

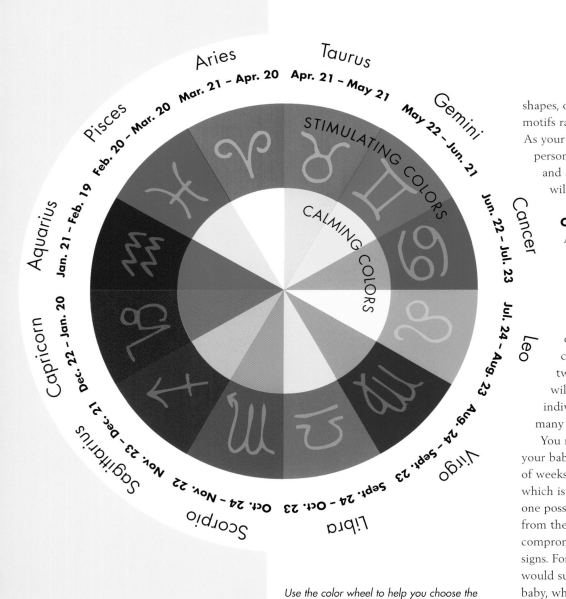

Use the color wheel to help you choose the most suitable colors for your baby's nursery or playroom.

shapes, or use stenciled or stamped motifs rather than freehand designs. As your baby grows up, these personal touches will mean a lot, and any lack of artistic expertise will be overlooked.

Colors of the zodiac

According to astrology, the sign under which your baby is born will determine many aspects of his personality, including which colors he will be attracted to. It is also thought that the date of birth has an influence on character and tastes. Although two babies born on the same day will each be widely differing individuals, they will also have many likes and dislikes in common. You may not know exactly when your baby will be born; allow a couple of weeks on either side of the due date, which is likely to give you more than one possible sign. However, as you'll see from the chart, you can often find a compromise between two neighboring signs. For example, a soft orangey-red would suit either a Pisces or an Aries baby, while a baby born under Virgo, Libra, or Scorpio would be attracted to medium to dark blues.

The outer edge of the wheel pictured opposite shows the more stimulating colors that appeal to those born under the sign in question, while the inner colors are the more calming ones appropriate to each sign of the zodiac.

Numerology and colors

An alternative approach to selecting colors for your baby's room is based on numbers. Numerology is another ancient system that defies scientific proof, and yet many people find it a reliable indicator of personality and taste.

To select a color for your baby using this technique, determine the baby's "personality number," using his name. If your baby isn't born yet and you don't know the sex, do it for your top-choice names for both a boy and a girl.

Each letter is assigned a number. Using your baby's first name, look at the chart below to find the number for each letter and then add all these together. If the resulting number has two or more digits, add these together. Keep doing this (if necessary) until you have a number between 1 and 9.

For example, suppose you are expecting a baby girl and plan to call her Megan. Her numbers would be: M = 4; E = 5; G = 7; A = 1; N = 5. This adds up to a total of 22. By adding 2 + 2 you get the final number, 4. This is the number for the name Megan.

Color chart

The chart above shows which colors are best suited to each of the numbers. So if your baby girl is named Megan, and therefore has 4 as her personality number, she should be very happy in a room that is decorated in green.

Numerology chart

1	2	3	4	5	6	7	8	9
A	B	C	D	E	F	G	H	I
J	K	L	M	N	O	P	Q	R
S	T	U	V	W	X	Y	Z	

Introducing color and light

Light ideas

Daylight is important to your baby, who will learn after a few weeks to tell the difference between night and day. Unless the room is already very light, make sure your curtains can be pulled right back off the windows so that you let in as much light as possible. You can also increase the amount of light in other ways, particularly by reflecting natural light. Mirrors are the obvious way to do this, but not the only one. Here are a few more light-reflecting ideas:

- Crystals hanging in the window
- Mobiles with reflective or glittery surfaces
- Shiny or reflective ornaments
- Wall decorations that incorporate shiny or reflective materials such as mirrors sewn into appliquéd hangings or a mosaic mural with opalescent tiles (check mosaics regularly to make sure no small tiles are coming loose)

As your baby acquires new toys, you can use these to reinforce the color scheme of his room. Let natural light flood into the nursery and try using pretty stained-glass stickers on the windows (see opposite).

We've looked at the basic color scheme of your baby's room and the colors of the walls and fabrics, but there are plenty of other opportunities to bring color into the room. Think about the colors whenever you choose any of the following items:

- Furniture and fittings
- Rugs
- Accessories
- Pictures, friezes, and wall hangings
- Crystals
- Mobiles
- Toys

Baby toys are a particularly good source of color and stimulation even when your baby is only looking and not touching. Have enough shelves to keep bright and attractive toys out on display instead of putting them all away.

Wall coverings

Blank, bare walls look stark and unwelcoming and contain nothing to stimulate your baby's developing senses. Decorate the walls with pictures or posters for your baby to look at. Wall hangings are a great way to brighten up a room and can bring in textures as well as colors. The softness of fabrics brings warmth to the room—something as simple as a baby's patchwork blanket can make a great wall hanging, or you could create your own abstract design out of old clothes in different colors and fabrics. If you're more artistically inclined, an embroidery or appliqué of animals, trains, or flowers can be fun as well as colorful.

Murals and hand-painted friezes are another good way to personalize the room and introduce color. These can be as modest or as ambitious as you like, and you can paint the whole room or just a cupboard door. A soft, gentle color scheme can be livened up with a brightly colored frieze. If you can't afford a lot of pictures for the walls, this is a great way to warm up the room and make it more interesting for your baby.

Using crystals

Which crystal to use?

Here are some of the crystals that you might like to use for your baby, along with their properties:

Amethyst	spiritual uplift
Beryl	protection
Bloodstone	creativity
Chrysoprase	spiritual protection
Coral	emotional security
Emerald	physical or emotional healing
Jade	relaxation
Malachite	harmony
Moonstone	balance
Mother-of-pearl	protection, mother's love
Opal	release of potential
Jasper	happiness
Rose quartz	calm and healing
Ruby	love

Opal

Chrysoprase

According to the principles of crystal therapy, precious and semiprecious stones have powerful properties we can tap into. The theory behind crystal therapy is that each crystal vibrates imperceptibly at its own rate. These vibrations interact with your own aura, or your baby's, if the gemstone is placed within a suitable range.

Each type of crystal has its own vibrational rate and therefore its own particular property. This means you can use crystals to bestow characteristics, luck, or protection on yourself or on your baby. It's all a matter of knowing which crystals to use and how to use them.

How to use crystals

The most common way for adults to use crystals is to wear them as jewelry, in a pouch around the neck, or tied at the waist. However, this may present a choking hazard for a baby, so you'll need to use a different method.

You can sew a crystal into a baby's clothes or favorite blanket, although it will need to be removed before you wash the clothing. It obviously must not be uncomfortable if your baby lies on it.

An alternative is to associate the crystal with somewhere your baby spends a lot of his time. You could suspend the crystal from a mobile over the crib, hang it in front of the nursery window, or keep it in a pouch (preferably silk or silk velvet) attached to your baby's cradle or car seat. When he grows older and outgrows his crib, you might like to have the crystal turned into a piece of jewelry so that your child can continue to wear it.

Whichever method you choose, take care to ensure the crystal won't present a danger to your baby.

Preparing crystals

The crystals should always be pure and unblemished. Make sure you're using the real thing and not dyed glass. Crystals can acquire negative energy, so they need to be cleansed before you use them. There are many different ways to cleanse a crystal:

• Leave it out in the sun for several hours. (However, sunlight damages some crystals, including amethyst, aquamarine, beryl, citrine, rose quartz, and sapphire.)
• Leave it in the moonlight overnight.
• Leave it out in the rain for a day.
• Bury it in moist sand (but take care this does not damage the surface of a polished crystal).
• Leave it on a horizontal mirror overnight.

- Place it in filtered or distilled water and leave overnight.
- Leave it in the freezer overnight.
- Soak it in salt water for several hours, then allow it to dry naturally.
- Soak it in sage tea for several hours, wash it in filtered or distilled water, and then allow it to dry naturally.
- Pass it through the smoke from burning incense such as sweet grass, sage, or cedar.
- Wash it in a river, stream, or the sea.

Which crystal to use?

You might also like to use a crystal that is associated with your baby's astrological sign. Here are suitable stones to use for each of the twelve signs:

Aries	jasper
Taurus	emerald
Gemini	tiger's eye
Cancer	moonstone
Leo	rock crystal
Virgo	citrine
Libra	sapphire
Scorpio	garnet
Sagittarius	topaz
Capricorn	lapis lazuli
Aquarius	turquoise
Pisces	aquamarine

Citrine

Moonstone

Your baby will enjoy watching the reflected light dancing from a hanging crystal.

The influence of sound

Motor noises

Many babies are attracted to mechanical sounds, from the kitchen blender to a helicopter flying over. If these noises are very loud or sudden, however, they may frighten him, but otherwise there's a good chance your baby will be as interested in motorcycles as in Mantovani.

Even though you might not think of a particular sound as being pleasant or interesting, your baby may be fascinated by it. Not only that, but babies can even be soothed by the most improbable noises. The sound (and movement) of the car engine is notoriously soporific for babies, but many little ones will happily fall asleep to the strains of the vacuum cleaner or the dryer.

All of your baby's senses need to be stimulated and that includes hearing. From music to gentle tinkling sounds or even the noise of the car engine, filling your baby's world with pleasant noises will help him to develop. There are many ways you can do this, including the following:
• Music
• Wind chimes (outside the window, unless the weather is very warm)
• Rain chimes (obviously outside the window, too)
• Natural sounds, such as the whistling of wind in the trees or running water
• Toys that play tunes or make interesting sounds

Voice of calm

Soothing sounds are important in comforting your baby. You will naturally talk or sing to him when he's fractious, and the sound of your voice will help him to feel safe and relaxed. Gentle rhythms and long, drawn-out vowel sounds have an instinctively calming effect on a small baby.

But what happens when you're not there? You are the ideal comforter, but your baby may want to continue to hear such soothing sounds while he goes to sleep or when he wakes during the night. In this case, you can play music to keep your baby happy. Lullabies soothe some babies, and others respond positively to recordings of womb sounds. You can also buy small units that attach to your baby's crib and are sound-activated to play soothing sounds whenever your baby stirs and cries.

Different babies respond to different sounds, so experiment to find out what helps your baby to relax and sleep.

Getting it recorded

There are all sorts of CDs you can buy to play to your baby, either for stimulation at playtime or to help him sleep at naptime or at night. Obviously you can play children's tunes and

Older babies love toys that play tunes, especially when they can push the buttons themselves.

Your baby can hear sounds inside the womb during the later months of pregnancy.

lullabies, jazz, and classical. Playing a variety of music will stimulate him during the day, but playing just a few tracks repeatedly so they rapidly become recognized will be more comforting for him when falling asleep.

Recordings of natural sounds, including womb noises, are available.

Some babies enjoy these sounds and quickly find security in their repetition. You can also record your own cassettes. You might, for example, record the sound of your own voice speaking comfortingly to your baby or perhaps record yourself playing an instrument or singing lullabies.

Movement in the nursery

Curtains blowing gently in the breeze can keep your baby fascinated for several minutes at a time.

Movement attracts babies from the first few days, even though it takes a few months before babies can really focus properly. Anything that moves will intrigue your baby, even your hand and fingers wiggling a few inches from his face. The closer an object is, the sooner your baby will be able to focus on it. However, more distant movement will still draw your baby's attention even when the object is indistinct.

One of the best ways to bring movement into the nursery is with light and its reflections and shadows. If you have natural light coming through the window that is filtered through tree branches, this is ideal. The flickering shadows will keep your baby fascinated for ages. Reflections of water on the walls and ceiling will have the same engaging effect.

Even without these natural benefits, you can introduce reflections with lighting and mirrors. Light will naturally bounce off mirrors, and if you hang reflective mobiles in the window, they will bounce patterns around the room.

Windows are an obvious source of movement because any wind outside will cause movement. Lightweight curtains will billow in the breeze through an open window, and wind chimes will swing and glitter. You can position your baby to see out the window and watch branches swaying in the wind.

Generating movement

As well as these natural sources of movement, there are ways to create it artificially. Televisions fascinate babies, not surprisingly, although you might not want to encourage your child to watch too much. Plenty of toys move, and babies will enjoy watching you operate such toys even before they can manage it themselves. A pull-along dog or a battery-driven toy train will stimulate your baby from his first few weeks.

It won't be long before he can make things move by himself. Baby gyms and clip-on toys swinging from somewhere above the baby give him the chance to create his own movement. As he tries to reach for such toys, he will bat them and cause them to move. As your baby grows, he will learn to open flaps, lift lids, and push buttons, opening up all sorts of avenues of exploration. All through this time—and beyond, as your baby grows into a toddler—he will be drawn to toys that move and will enjoy generating the movement itself.

Mobile fascination

Babies love mobiles. They can enjoy mobiles when they are lying down, providing a source of enjoyment even if you have left the room. A mobile above your baby's crib will often mesmerize him as he relaxes for sleep, and keep him happily engaged until his eyes close and he drifts off.

All sorts of mobiles are available today, including those with lights, those that play music, and those that are glittery. You can also buy units that attach to the crib and project pictures or moving lights onto the ceiling.

Another way to interest your child through movement as he falls asleep is with a revolving night-light. These lights, with low-wattage bulbs, have a slowly rotating cylinder around the bulb that the light shines through, illuminating the picture on it.

Combining the effects

Using the best of nature

In good weather, your baby will enjoy being outdoors. There are plenty of sensory stimuli to interest babies and many that will mesmerize and send them off to sleep. Sounds such as birds singing or running water, if you live in a quiet area, will interest your child. In an urban setting, many babies will happily fall asleep to the sound of traffic or lawn mowers.

At the same time as your baby listens to these sounds, he can see trees and plants swaying in the breeze, birds and airplanes flying overhead, or cars going past. If you can put your baby in the shade of a tree, he will be absorbed by the sound of the breeze in the leaves and the patterns of the sun filtering through the branches.

Wind chimes can combine sound, movement, color, and light to entrance your baby.

Movement, color, light, sound: All of these stimulate your child or can be used to soothe him to sleep. And you don't have to choose just one—there are lots of objects that will appeal to more than one of your baby's senses to increase his mental stimulation or emotional relaxation.

Stimulating the senses

Many moving objects stimulate, so combining these with ones that make sounds is bound to fascinate your baby, whether it is a music box with a revolving statue inside or a brightly colored musical mobile. Wind chimes, which jangle together as they move in the breeze, are intriguing to a baby, especially metal wind chimes with their reflective, shiny surfaces. Babies also love to watch moving, colored lights, such as lava lamps or color-changing fiber optics.

Soothing your baby

Although you want to maintain your child's interest in the world around him until he falls asleep, you don't want to overstimulate him so that he finds it harder to go to sleep. You should therefore aim for:

- Softer colors
- Dimmer lights
- Gentler movement
- Quieter sounds

Any kind of gently moving, low-level light will help to calm your baby until his eyes close. Lullaby music played on a mobile will help get him off to sleep, especially in a soft-colored room with dim lighting to create a calm sanctuary.

Watching older children

If you have other children, don't overlook them as the best source of stimulation for your baby. They move, they make a noise, and they are usually bright and interesting to look at. Babies are fascinated by other children even more than by adults. If you don't have older children of your own, find opportunities for your baby to spend time around your friends' children.

Not only will he be happily entertained for hours watching the older children, but it's also the best way for him to learn about the next stages of development for himself. Toddlers and young children often have a natural rapport with babies. Do everything you can to encourage your older children's natural interest in their new baby brother or sister.

Spiritual ornaments

Dream catchers are used by many Native Americans. They believe that these nets are magical—capturing any bad dreams before they reach the sleeper and only letting the happy ones through.

5
Aromatherapy
and
the senses

The benefits of touch

Touch and feel

You can encourage your child to enjoy touch and texture by dressing her in fabrics that feel attractive to the touch, giving her soft, fleecy blankets, and encouraging her to play with toys of many different textures. Your child will learn from touching hard, cold, or rough materials as well as soft, warm, and smooth ones, so long as they won't actually hurt her. You can buy "touch and feel" baby books, which have a variety of textures for your baby to explore.

Babies enjoy exploring the feel of different textures.

Touch is very important to babies. It's not just a pleasurable sensation; it's an intrinsic part of their development. It is their primary sense when they are first born, the only one that has been given full rein in the womb. Babies need to cuddle, be rocked, and feel the warmth of another body, just as they have grown used to doing before birth.

Skin to skin

For any mother who chooses to breast-feed, this is the perfect opportunity to give her baby close physical contact through both body and mouth. If your baby isn't breast-fed, bottle-feeding is still a great time for cuddling and giving warmth and security. The most beneficial type of touch of all for babies is direct skin-to-skin contact. While this is a natural part of breast-feeding, it isn't an automatic part of life for bottle-fed babies, so it's worth bearing in mind that your baby needs this form of touch.

You can give your baby direct skin contact if you share a bed, or by taking the baby into the bath with you instead of always using the baby bath. And, of course, warm weather gives you the opportunity to strip down to sunbathing gear and have lots of cuddles with your baby, who can happily wear nothing but a diaper, if that. Just make sure to stay in the shade.

The culture of touch

In the West, we tend to put our babies down much of the time, in a Moses basket, a crib, a car seat, or whatever. We get on with other jobs while we can, and whenever we have a spare moment, we talk to the baby, stimulate her, rock her, entertain her. If the baby is fussing, we may try to carry her around and get on with tasks while we look after her.

In most non-Westernized cultures, however, babies are treated in the opposite way. If a mother holds her baby almost constantly, looking after the baby isn't so much a task (however pleasant) as something that happens unthinkingly as the mother goes about her daily life. These babies are rarely given any direct, focused attention, but are constantly touched and held. In some cultures, the baby is never put down at all, being carried by day and sleeping beside the mother at night.

The Ache tribe, who live in the jungles of Paraguay, have been found to hold their babies ninety-three percent of the time during the day, as well as all through the night. In some cultures, babies are swaddled to their mothers for the first few months, and in many others they are carried almost continuously in slings. Such babies seem to thrive on minimal direct attention but maximum physical contact.

This kind of touch-focused upbringing for a baby means that instead of the mother being frustrated by a baby's constant demands to be held or fed, such demands are met unconsciously before they can even be made. There is no thought of training a baby to go through the night without a feeding, or settle to sleep on her own. She is encouraged to sleep and feed at will, being always in contact with her mother or a close adult caregiver.

Even when asleep, your baby still benefits from your touch.

Massage for babies

Go with the flow

The guidelines below suggest a massage routine for your baby. However, don't feel bound by this. It doesn't matter at all if you know nothing about massage. Just spending the time touching and focusing on her is beneficial. The only important guidelines to follow are:

- Be firm but gentle.
- Create a relaxing rhythm.
- Always massage toward the heart (following the direction of the circulation).
- Don't massage the baby's hands, as the oil could be transferred to her mouth.
- Don't massage an immunization site for forty-eight hours after the baby has had the shot. After this, massage may help to break down any residual lump.
- Never massage directly on the spine; keep your fingers on either side of the spinal column.

Massaging your baby is a great way for both of you to bond and feel physically close. As well as the beneficial effects of touch for babies, regular massage also helps them feed and sleep better and can ease colic and constipation. Other studies have shown that massage has such diverse benefits as making babies more alert and responsive, reducing anxiety, and helping them absorb food more effectively.

Creating the right mood

It's no good massaging your baby when you're feeling stressed or are in a rush, or when your baby is hungry, tired, or unsettled. You need to create a relaxing, happy atmosphere for the massage to be successful. It's a good idea to massage your baby at a regular time of day that works for both of you, such as midmorning or after bathtime before she goes to sleep at night.

Make eye contact and talk or sing to your baby during the massage in order to maximize the physical contact and involvement, and create a secure and happy environment. It won't be long before she learns to enjoy these sessions and to recognize when you're beginning a massage. If ever she really isn't in the mood, abandon the massage and do it

later; there's no point forcing it when the time isn't right.

You can massage your baby indoors, but if the weather is warm, why not go outside in the shade? Since she will be looking upward, make sure the light isn't too bright. An outdoor massage makes it more practical to remove your baby's diaper, and the sensations of warm air and maybe a gentle breeze on the skin will add to her enjoyment.

There are several practical and safety considerations to keep in mind when you massage your baby. These are the main guidelines:

- Don't give a massage immediately after a feeding.
- Since you will need to remove your baby's clothes, make sure you're in a warm enough room.
- Ideally, remove her diaper as well. However, you can leave it on if you prefer.
- Remove any jewelry that might hurt her, and check that your nails are short enough not to scratch.
- If you're called away for any reason, don't leave your baby alone on a bed or changing table. Take her with you.
- Remember that once your baby is covered in a thin layer of oil, she can be very slippery. If you need to pick her up,

be careful and wrap her in a towel first.
• The right length of time for a baby massage is about ten minutes—you'll sense when your baby has had enough.

Preparing for the massage

Before you begin the massage, have everything you need ready:
• Towel
• Massage oil
• Clean diaper
• Clean clothes

Your baby needs to be lying down for the massage. Lay out a clean towel on a flat surface. You can stand up and massage your baby on a changing mat at table height, or you might prefer to sit on the floor or on a bed with your legs stretched out in front of you. Put the towel over your legs, and then put the baby on top of the towel.

Front massage

1 Lay your baby on her back to begin the massage, with her feet toward you.
2 Put a small amount of oil in one hand and rub your hands together. Put one hand on each of her ankles, and run your hands firmly up to the tops of her legs. Bring them back gently touching your baby's legs, but exerting no pressure as your hands move down her legs. Do this four or five times.
3 Hold each foot with your hands, supporting the top of the feet and the ankles with your fingers so that your thumbs are in contact with the soles. Massage with your thumbs in circles, clockwise and then counterclockwise, four or five times.
4 Run one hand right up your baby's legs to her tummy, and massage this in a

Gentle massage is good for your baby physically, mentally, and emotionally.

Massage oil for babies

Ideally, use grapeseed oil, almond oil, or a blend of four parts almond oil and one part jojoba oil as a base oil. You can add essential oils to this, but only in very small quantities. Don't use more than two drops of essential oil to every ½ cup.

Not all essential oils are suitable for babies, but the following are safe in the small quantities outlined:

- Roman chamomile
- Rose
- Neroli
- Lavender

If your baby suffers from colic or constipation, use a drop of tangerine or mandarin oil.

clockwise, circular motion a few times (this is particularly useful if your baby has colic or is constipated).

5 Now move both hands up to the shoulders and then slide them loosely down the arms to the wrists.

6 Massage the baby's arms from wrists to shoulders in the same way that you massaged the legs.

7 Hold the baby's wrists and bring her arms together across her chest, then lay them back at the sides again. Repeat three or four times.

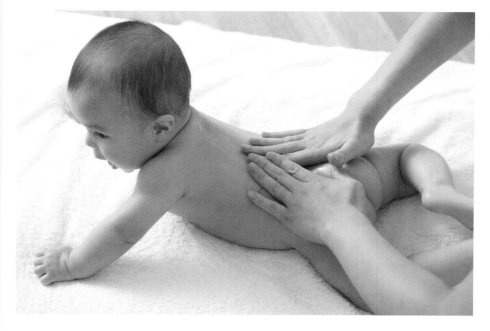

Back massage

You can now turn the baby over and massage her while she is lying on her stomach (see below). Many babies don't like this position, however. If yours doesn't, don't worry—just don't massage in this position. But if your baby is happy on her front, here's how to do a massage in this position:

1 Massage the backs of the legs in the same way as you massaged the front—from ankles to buttocks, gliding your hands gently. Repeat three or four times.

Many babies find a gentle face massage relaxing and enjoyable.

2 Now run your hands up your baby's back, either side of the spine, from bottom to shoulders. Repeat three or four times.
3 Finally, massage the shoulders gently upward along the line of the shoulder blades. Repeat three or four times.

Face massage

Many babies enjoy having a face massage. Never use oil for this, and be very gentle, especially around the fontanelle. Hold the baby's head with one hand and massage one side of the face with the other hand, then swap sides.
1 Stroke from the top of the nose out across the forehead in a semicircle.
2 Stroke down the side of the face past the ear and around the jaw (see above).
3 Bring your fingertips back up, skirting the side of the mouth, to run up along the edge of the nose.
4 Repeat three or four times and then change hands.
5 Change hands back again and stroke lightly with your fingertips from the bridge of the nose across the top of the head, taking great care to be extremely gentle across the fontanelle.
6 Repeat three or four times and then change hands.

Natural sensations

Enjoy your own backyard

Babies love being outdoors as long as the weather is warm enough for them, or they're snugly wrapped up. Even if you have a very small backyard, you can still put your baby outside for a daytime nap in the summer, rather than in the nursery. Adults enjoy snoozing in the sunshine, so it's no surprise that babies enjoy it, too. The experience is a very sensual one. Even if you have no garden at all, you can put your baby beside an open window indoors when the weather suits (provided she is not yet mobile enough to be able to climb up to it).

You'll need to fix up some kind of shade for your baby, unless the garden has its own natural shade. Babies' skin can burn even through some fabrics, so use a reliably protective sunshade if the sun is very hot. You'll also need to keep an eye out to protect your baby from cats and dogs and any other local wildlife that might disturb her.

There are few more pleasurable sensations for a baby (or an adult, for that matter) than those that come naturally. Although you need to keep your baby safe and warm, don't cosset her or wrap her up so well that she can't appreciate the world around her. Give your baby every opportunity to enjoy the sensations that surround her outdoors.

Visit different locations with your baby in order to give her the benefit of the varying experiences on offer. Take her into the garden to enjoy the sensation of warm sunshine on the skin (obviously you need to do this on a day when the sun isn't strong enough to burn her delicate skin). Go for a walk on a windy hillside and let the wind blow through your baby's hair. A visit to the beach is a good time to take off your baby's shoes and let her feel the sand between her toes. Or go to a stream or lake on a warm day and hold her so she can dabble her toes in the water.

Feel as you walk

When you take your baby for a walk, encourage her to feel some of the more interesting textures around. Pick up objects and brush them against her cheek or hold her hand and help her to stroke or touch them. This kind of experience will broaden your baby's mind, and sharing the exercise with you will make it safe and even more exciting. As your baby gets a little older, you can encourage her to hold and feel things for herself, so long as you make sure she doesn't put them in her mouth.

Some of the objects you might find for your baby to touch and feel include:
- Feathers
- Leaves
- Stones
- Grasses
- Moss

As well as textures, you can demonstrate different temperatures to your baby by showing her the heat of a sun-baked stone or the cool of the water in a stream. And don't forget the sounds that go with the feel of things—the crackle of dead leaves, the whisper of grasses, or the babbling of water.

Even when you're in the house, you can still broaden your baby's experience by showing her the feel of the water, or the breeze through an open window.

Your baby will enjoy the sensations of being outside and exploring nature's textures.

Aromatherapy

This is all about using smells to treat ailments or to improve and lift our emotional state. It is commonly associated with massage but, in fact, while massage is certainly a popular way of using aromatherapy, it is by no means the only way.

Aromatherapy is a valuable tool throughout pregnancy and birth, and for your baby, too. Regular aromatherapy will help to create a relaxed, calm mother and baby, which in turn helps the two of you to bond strongly.

Using essential oils

Essential oils are highly concentrated plant oils used in aromatherapy. Different essential oils have their own distinct effects, so they can induce different responses in us according to which we use. They work either through our sense of smell or through being absorbed into the skin.

Since essential oils are strong and concentrated, they can harm sensitive skin when used in significant amounts. They are therefore always used in a very diluted form if they are going to come into contact with the skin. This is especially true with babies, on whom undiluted essential oils should never be used. When the oil is diluted in a carrier or base oil such as sweet almond or grapeseed oil, it can be applied directly to the skin using massage. It can take up to seven hours for the skin to absorb these oils fully, so it's best not to bathe or shower during this time.

Many essential oils are particularly useful during pregnancy and after childbirth for helping to repair the body and get it back to full fitness quickly. Some of the best oils include:
- Lavender (relaxing, good for the skin, eases headaches and other aches and pains)
- Mandarin or tangerine (calming and cheering)
- Neroli (peaceful, good for the skin—including reducing stretch marks)
- Petitgrain (soothing, eases depression)
- Ylang-ylang (eases tension and worry)

Using aromatherapy

The classic way to use aromatherapy is to be given a massage by a qualified aromatherapy masseuse. However, you can derive just as much benefit from the oils in a number of other ways. Many of these are suitable for both you and your baby. While certain oils are most helpful to mothers to ease physical ailments in pregnancy and after the birth, many are valuable for fathers, too. Essential oils

It is important to choose a suitable base or carrier oil for essential oils.

Carrier oils

You'll need a carrier or base oil to dilute the essential oils if you're applying them directly to your skin. Good carrier oils to use during pregnancy include:
- Avocado
- Grapeseed
- Jojoba
- Sweet almond
- Wheatgerm

that ease stress and promote relaxation are worthwhile for the whole family.

Doing an aromatherapy massage yourself is perfectly feasible—you don't have to be an expert to know what feels good. You and your partner or a friend can easily massage back and shoulders. A foot massage, or foot and leg massage, is also very welcome during pregnancy. A face massage can be extremely relaxing, too. Make sure your face is clean and free of makeup before you start.

There are just a few safety guidelines to follow for home massages:
- Avoid massaging the lower back or abdomen.
- Always massage toward the heart.
- Don't massage directly over varicose veins.
- Don't have a massage if you are experiencing any bleeding.
- Avoid lying on your stomach if you are more than three months pregnant.

Another great way to use aromatherapy is to put three or four drops of essential oil into a bath, swooshing the water around to mix it in. Use either a refreshing oil to start the day or a relaxing oil to help you sleep at the end of the day. A single drop of oil is all you should use in a baby's bath, and then only after three months of age.

You can inhale the smell of aromatherapy oils by putting a few drops in hot water, then sitting with your head over the water and a towel over your head for up to five minutes. Children and babies shouldn't inhale in this way, but you can place a bowl of hot water with a drop or two of oil in the room with them.

A drop of oil on a tissue, which you can sniff when you need to, is another good way of using aromatherapy. Or put a drop of relaxing oil such as lavender on your pillow. Neither of these techniques should be used with babies, however, as their skin is too delicate to risk coming into direct contact with essential oils.

There are several ways to fill a room with scent from oils. You can buy oil burners, lightbulb rings, or diffusers to spread the scent by heating the oils. Homemade variations on this theme are also possible:
- Put a few drops of oil on a cotton ball and put it behind the radiator (out of your baby's reach).
- Put the scented cotton balls in the vacuum cleaner to perfume each room you vacuum.
- Put half a dozen drops of oil in a

Oils to avoid

Certain essential oils should not be used when you are pregnant. The following list is not exhaustive; if you're unsure, don't use any oil until you've checked it out with a qualified aromatherapist or your doctor. Here are some common aromatherapy oils to steer clear of during pregnancy:
- Basil
- Cedarwood
- Clary sage
- Clove
- Cinnamon
- Fennel
- Jasmine
- Juniper
- Marjoram
- Oregano
- Peppermint
- Rosemary
- Sage
- Thyme

plant mister full of water. Shake it and then spray the mister around the room.

Aromatherapy for babies
Aromatherapy can help your baby to feel calmer and more settled. For babies, aromatherapy certainly shouldn't replace conventional medical treatment, but it can complement it. It's also invaluable for those minor problems that don't warrant calling a doctor but do make your baby unhappy, such as teething, minor sniffles, or mild diaper rash. However, if it is anything more than a very minor ailment, or you are in any doubt at all, call a doctor.

Essential oils
The following essential oils are all safe for use with a baby, so long as they are always used sparingly and don't come into direct contact with your baby's skin:
- Eucalyptus (antiseptic and anti-inflammatory)
- Lavender (relaxing and for minor skin problems and bruises)
- Lemon (refreshing and antiseptic)
- Mandarin or tangerine (calming and cheering)
- Tea tree (good for skin complaints)
- Roman chamomile (antiseptic, anti-inflammatory, and antispasmodic)

A drop of essential oil in your baby's bath can help with minor ailments.

Aromatherapy solutions

Blocked nose   Add two or three drops of essential oil to a vaporizer, diffuser, or oil burner or simply to a bowl of hot water (out of the baby's reach). Use lavender, lemon, or eucalyptus.

Bruises   Make a cold compress by adding two drops of lavender oil to one cup of cold water and mixing well. Lay a washcloth on top of the water to collect the oils. Squeeze it out well and place it on the bruise, without applying pressure or massaging it in. Repeat as necessary.

Constipation   Massage the lower back and abdomen in circular, clockwise movements two or three times a day (diaper-changing time is the obvious time to do it). Use a carrier oil that contains a drop or two of Roman chamomile oil.

Cradle cap   Add one or two drops of tea tree oil to a 2 fl. oz. bottle of baby shampoo. Use it sparingly, and avoid contact with eyes.

Diarrhea   If this is severe, you should seek medical treatment urgently. But in mild cases, you can use aromatherapy. Dilute two drops of lavender oil in a little whole milk and add it to your baby's bath.

Diaper rash   Add one drop of Roman chamomile oil to three tablespoons of sweet almond oil. Apply a small amount to the area at diaper-changing time.

Teething   Use one or two drops of lavender oil in a vaporizer or oil burner in your baby's room, or just in a bowl of hot water.

Insomnia   If an older baby has trouble falling asleep, a relaxing bath can help. One or two drops of lavender or Roman chamomile oil diluted in a little whole milk will make the bathwater more soothing. Don't use this with babies under three months old.

Always use an extrasoft sponge on your baby as her skin is very delicate and needs gentle care.

Natural scents

Real food

Smell is an important part of eating for older children and adults. Think of how your taste buds are stimulated by the smell of a delicious meal cooking. Babies are equally able to enjoy the smells associated with food; they have a highly developed ability to smell their mother's milk as soon as they're born.

Your baby can be encouraged to enjoy food smells if you give her fresh foods once you wean her onto solids. Jars and packages of food are getting healthier all the time—you can now buy organic fruit purees in jars—but they still don't compare with the real thing. It is much more exciting for your baby to smell the apples stewing on the stove or the fresh banana as you peel open the skin.

You may not always have time to cook fresh foods for your baby every day, but try to give them to her as often as you can and let her smell the food cooking or being prepared. She will enjoy the anticipation of scrumptious foods as much as you do.

You can introduce your baby to all sorts of smells through aromatherapy. But don't forget, too, the impact of natural fragrances on your baby's senses. Smell is one of the most highly developed senses at birth, and babies will respond to new smells from their first few days, especially girls (baby boys also develop their sense of smell early, but it isn't so sensitive).

Encourage a baby to explore scents with strong-smelling objects such as pinecones, or by dipping a cotton swab in different scents and holding it under the baby's nose. Babies are less inclined than adults to differentiate between "good" and "bad" smells but will respond to the stimulation of new smells. You can encourage this exploration with scents such as:
- Vanilla
- Pinecones
- Seaweed
- Flowers
- Baking bread

Scented flowers give a wide range of perfumes and are an obvious and ideal source of interesting smells to introduce your baby to. Keep scented flowers in the house, and take her around the garden or the park trying out smells. Hold her close to the scented flower, but make sure she can't grab any thorny stems or pull off leaves and petals to stuff in her mouth. Remember, too, that many plants have leaves that are aromatic when crushed.

If you're thinking of growing scented plants, here are some of the best for your baby to enjoy:
- Honeysuckle
- Jonquils
- Lavender
- Lilac
- Lilies
- Dianthus
- Roses
- Sweet peas

Many herbs have aromatic leaves, which you can crush so that your baby can smell them better. For example:
- Curry plant
- Fennel
- Lemon balm
- Oregano
- Rosemary
- Thyme

The natural world is bursting
with fragrance and aromas—try
to encourage your baby to
discover them.

6

The
power of thought
and action

Positive thinking

Baby blues

It's estimated that two in three mothers experience a couple of days of tearfulness in the first ten days after giving birth. Most commonly kicking in around day three, it usually lasts no more than forty-eight hours.

Just because it's common and transient, however, is no reason to put up with it. There's plenty you can do to ease the baby blues, and before you know it, they'll have passed. Here are some suggestions:

- Wash your hair, even if free time for such things is at a premium. It will make you feel a lot better.
- Try to get a little exercise and fresh air, even just going for a walk. It's an immediate rejuvenator.
- Invite friends around to see you (and the new baby); human contact is a great preventative to feeling blue.
- Sleep whenever the baby does. You'll have a lot of sleep to catch up on.
- If this is your first baby, try not to get stressed about learning to look after him. If he's warm enough and well fed and you don't drop him, you're doing fine. It doesn't matter if you can't remember exactly how much cotton you're supposed to use or that you have to cover the baby in a towel because you can't remember where you put the baby blankets. Enjoy the learning process and don't worry.

Your attitude and feelings toward your baby and your new lifestyle will have a deep impact on your baby and your family. Harnessing the power of positive thoughts will enable you to create a sense of love and happiness in yourself, which will transfer to your baby.

The first few weeks after birth can be especially tiring, as your baby feeds frequently and barely seems to distinguish between day and night. Many women find it hard to be cheerful during this period, even though they are very happy with the new baby. If you're on your own a lot, this can be a tricky time. Equally, if you're also busy—especially looking after older children—you can easily become exhausted.

A positive attitude may sometimes seem hard to muster, but it's worth the effort. You will be able to enjoy this precious time with your baby, and your baby will benefit immeasurably from the happy atmosphere. Babies and children are very sensitive to moods and will sense if things aren't right.

Looking up

However tough it is, try to find some time for yourself to help you develop a more positive approach. Get someone else to take care of the baby (and any

other children) for even just half an hour a day. If your baby goes to sleep at a reasonable hour, perhaps you could take some time once he's asleep.

Do something that makes you feel positive and happy. This might mean relaxing with a good book or a warm bath, or it could mean going for a walk. Some people find it therapeutic to spend some time in the garden, perhaps picking flowers. Maybe you miss work, and half an hour's work each day will give your brain the stimulation it needs. You might want to listen to loud music, or maybe you feel better just having time to put on some makeup and face the day feeling more human.

Good company

One of the biggest causes of depression in the first few months after childbirth is isolation. Delightful as babies are, they are not the most stimulating conversationalists. One in five mothers suffers postpartum depression, and many of them have little contact with other adults for much of the day. It doesn't always feel easy to get out of the house with a new baby in tow, and if depression sets in, it becomes even harder to mobilize yourself.

Whether you're suffering from postpartum depression or simply feeling low from time to time, make sure you spend plenty of time with other people to help you stay cheerful and positive. Here are some ideas:

- Join a mother-and-baby group.
- Talk to friends on the phone if it's hard to get out and see them—you can do this while you're feeding your baby.
- Make sure you socialize regularly, even if you don't always feel like it.
- Try to do things with other mothers, even if it's only the weekly shopping.
- Tell your partner how you're feeling; don't suffer in silence.
- If you're too tired to cook, invite friends over and get take-out.

An occasional shopping trip, ideally with friends, is a great reason to get out of the house with your new baby.

Talking to your baby

Contact on the move

It can be quite tricky communicating with your baby while you're on the go. Supermarket shopping is great because the seats in the carts bring your baby close to your eye level and facing you, so you can chat to him as you go around. But what if you're cooking or cleaning or doing paperwork?

One solution is to put your baby in a sling. This means both your hands are free, and the close physical contact will comfort him and keep him happy. You can then chat away as you cook or vacuum or pay bills. Just be careful to keep the baby away from anything dangerous such as hot cooking fat.

If you find a sling problematic, you can still improve contact with your baby by sitting him up in a car seat or rocker as you go about your chores. This allows you to maintain eye contact and talk more easily.

Talking directly to your baby is the key to teaching him to talk.

Language is one of the most vital aspects of your child's development, and one that everyone can encourage. The sooner your baby learns to talk, the less frustration he will experience. Two-way communication relies on learning speech.

The process of learning language begins as soon as a baby is born, even though it may be twelve months or more before he utters his first words. And your baby will learn to talk by being talked to. Listening to other people talking among themselves, or to the radio or television, is no help in teaching a child to speak—communication must be directed at the baby.

So to give your baby the stimulation he needs in order to learn to communicate, talk to him as much as you can. Chat to him in the car, talk as you go out for walks, and include him in conversations with the family.

What do you talk about?

A few people find it easy to chat away to babies. Most of us, however, wonder what to say to them. We're not really used to holding one-sided conversations and we don't know how to do it.

Here are some of the best ways to talk to your baby, which will help to stimulate him, make him feel loved, and encourage him to develop:

• Make frequent eye contact with your baby so you are communicating with him rather than talking into space. Facial expressions and gestures will follow automatically if you do this.

• You may find yourself talking in a higher pitch than you do to other people. Go with it; adults instinctively do this because babies find it easier to hear the higher frequency.

• Use normal, clear speech to your baby, and don't slip into the "oochie coochie coo" style of baby talk.

• Tell your baby what you're doing. Give him a running commentary, like a TV chef does. For example, "I'm just sorting out the white from the colored clothes because I don't want my white things to turn red. Then I put them in through this door here, shut the door, and turn this dial here."

• When something catches your baby's attention, tell him the name of the object: "That's a spoon. A spoon."

• After a few months, introduce adjectives into your talking. So instead of saying, "Look at that car," say, "Look at that red car," or, "Look at that fast car."

• Use repetition. Whether it's nursery rhymes, songs, or general chatting, babies love to hear sounds they recognize.

• Keep your language simple so your baby can understand it as easily as possible. But don't make it so simple that it doesn't stretch him. Babies don't have to understand every word—and in the first few months they won't—but as they get older, babies can understand a great deal more than they can show.

• You can start looking at picture books with a baby who's only a couple of months old. See what captures his interest and tell him the names of the objects he is looking at.

• Play games like peekaboo and "This little piggy went to market" with your baby. Diaper-changing time and bathtime are great opportunities to do this.

• Give your baby the opportunity to reply. Even gurgling or blowing bubbles is a way for him to learn about taking turns in conversation and lets you show him that you are listening to him.

You'll help your baby's language skills develop if you give him a running commentary on whatever you're doing, including household chores.

Blessings and rituals

Write a blessing for your baby and keep it safe.

You can make a set of angel cards special for your baby by personalizing it.

Special blessings and rituals are a way of harnessing positive thoughts and focusing them toward your baby. They help you to direct this energy toward whatever aspect of your baby's life you wish. You can use blessings and rituals to bring happiness, give protection, or bestow feelings of love on your baby.

Rituals are used around the world to mark the birth of a new baby. It is an important moment in your own life, and the very first in the baby's, so it's appropriate to celebrate the occasion. Here are a few ideas:

• Plant a tree. Choose one that you particularly like and that you feel is in some way appropriate. You might pick an oak to represent steadfastness and strength, or a fruit tree to symbolize your baby's life developing and bearing fruit. You might like to plant the placenta beneath the tree to fertilize it and also to personalize it to your baby.

• Bless your baby by touching his forehead with water that has been purified by leaving it overnight with a suitable crystal in it (see page 68).

• Write a permanent blessing for your baby (you can follow some of the ideas on these pages). Inscribe it or have it written by a calligrapher on a sheet of parchment. Roll it into a scroll and tie it with a ribbon. Keep it somewhere safe, and give it to your child for his eighteenth birthday.

• Give your baby a gift. Think of something significant, which will be meaningful to your baby when he grows up. You could choose anything from a bottle of vintage wine destined for his twenty-first birthday to a leather pouch filled with angel cards.

Naming the baby

Among the most important rituals associated with babies around the world is the naming ritual. Organized religions have their own naming ceremonies, often involving water for baptism. But if you don't follow an organized religion, you can still hold your own naming ceremony. Humanist organizations can give you ideas, or you can simply devise your own ceremony.

A suitable form for this to take is to invite people who will be important in the baby's life. Choose a location that you feel is appropriate, somewhere outdoors. The central part of the ritual entails whispering in your baby's right ear, "Your name is (baby's name)." three times. Then say aloud, "I name this baby (baby's name)." and then make a vow as parents, spoken together or one at a

Planting a tree and naming it after your baby is a lovely way to mark his birth. The tree symbolizes your hopes for the baby—that he will grow strong and healthy.

time. You can write your own vow, but here's an example: "I promise to be patient and kind with you, and to give you the best start in life that I can. I will support and protect you, and I will help and allow you to be yourself. Above all I will love you unconditionally." You may want other key members of the family, such as siblings and grandparents, to make vows as well.

After this, ask the blessing of Mother Earth for your baby, touching your baby's forehead to the ground and saying, "Bless this baby, (baby's name), and give him/her a long and happy life."

This is the basic ritual, but, as with a wedding, you might also want to have music and readings before and after. Just as religious ceremonies ask godparents to make a commitment to the baby, you can ask "mentors" to pledge their lifelong support to your child.

Do-it-yourself rituals

Either use prescribed blessings and rituals, or design your own. Any objects you use should symbolize the blessing so that it emphasizes the positive thoughts you are directing. For example, water might symbolize purity, or you could use a blue ribbon to denote calm, since blue is a calming color.

The important thing is that you focus on the desired outcome of the ritual, and any object should help you do this—that's why it's there. Write yourself a script, with words and actions, which symbolize what you are trying to achieve.

Suppose you are planting a tree, for example, to mark your baby's birth. Without a ritual, you might run out into the garden and plant the tree quickly before it rains—and anyway, you've got to go out shopping. In fact, you might run through the shopping list in your head as you were planting the tree. The purpose of a ritual is to make sure that as you plant the tree you focus on how you want your baby to grow strong and healthy like the tree, and on what kind of adult he might grow into.

So a tree-planting ritual could entail gathering your close family around and spending time digging the hole for the tree as you speak a few words about how the soil symbolizes the family that your new baby will grow in and that will nurture him. As you plant the tree, you could give it the same name as your baby. Tell the tree that you want it to grow strong and healthy, and that you will love and support it.

Baby showers

You can hold a baby shower either before or after the birth. If you hold it afterward, it is an important ritual for marking the baby's arrival. Although a baby shower is traditionally arranged by someone else, you could ask a grandparent, sister, or friend to organize it for you.

There's really no reason why you shouldn't throw your own baby shower. If the object of the exercise is to mark the birth rather than to be given presents, you can always make it clear on the invitation that you are not expecting gifts (this is a particularly good idea for a second or subsequent baby).

You might go for the traditional women-only shower, or follow the more modern route of holding a mixed baby shower. If you have asked people not to bring you baby-related paraphernalia as gifts, they will probably bring a present for the baby himself instead. If you have planned a naming ceremony for your baby, you can combine this with the baby shower.

Visualization

This is a powerful way of blessing your baby. All you need to do is to sit or lie with your eyes closed and draw a strong visual image in your mind of the blessing you want. For example, here's a visualization for bringing happiness to your baby.

Imagine your baby lying safely in his crib. Now see the sun outside the window. Rays of pink and yellow light are streaming out of the sun and in through the window of your baby's room. They are filling the whole room with pink and yellow and orange rays of happiness, crowding for space, and the colored lights are playing over the crib and around your baby as he sleeps.

The symbolism of a candle flame to represent the soul is common around the world.

Candle power

A single flame is a common symbol throughout the world for the human soul. You can incorporate a candle into your blessings and rituals to represent your baby's spiritual self.

A candle also represents protection. You can purify the whole room at nighttime by carrying a lit candle around it. As you leave the room, stand in the doorway and hold the candle up. Say a few words of blessing to your baby, as simple as, "Bless you, sleep safe," before you go. However, be careful with the open flame and have your baby cared for elsewhere while you perform blessings or purification rituals.

Ritual blessing

One of the most loving and comforting bedtime rituals is a good-night blessing. This is a ritual you can continue for several years—a personalized good night that not only blesses your child but quickly becomes familiar to him and so represents security and safety, too.

All you need to do is devise a few words to say to your baby at bedtime, as your way of saying good night. Choose words to tell him how much you love him, and end by blessing him. The most valuable blessing will be the one you compose yourself, but here are a couple of examples to give you an idea:

- "You are the most precious baby in the world and I love you more than anything. I will always be here to look after you. Good night, sleep safe, and bless you."
- "I love you every minute and every hour. I love you all day and all night. I love you every season and every year. I love you with all the love in the world, forever and beyond. Bless you from now until morning."

You can have fun with this blessing. Repeat it to your baby in a singsong voice (which babies love), so that he quickly starts to recognize the words even before he can understand them. The familiarity of the blessing and the eye contact with you as you say it will help him feel loved and secure. As he grows older, your child will learn what the words mean, and you can recite the blessing together.

Create a personalized blessing to repeat to your baby each night.

Staying cheerful

The chief causes of negativity when you have a small baby are stress, fatigue, and isolation. It follows that if you want to stay cheerful, you need to do what you can to counteract these factors.

Stress has lots of causes (including fatigue), but the key symptom is that you feel worried and tense; relaxation is therefore important. Your happiness is essential to your baby's well-being, so finding time to relax and de-stress is not selfish or unreasonable—it is key to looking after your baby well.

Do whatever you can to make time for yourself. Accept offers to look after the baby, get some paid help if necessary, and let your partner do his share. Then take a bath, go for a walk, catch up on sleep, or do whatever it is you need to do in order to stay relaxed and happy.

Make sure you plan plenty of socializing into your calendar so that you don't become lonely and isolated, but try to avoid a busy schedule that doesn't allow you to sleep. Socialize during the day or with people who don't expect you to party into the wee hours. There is no sleeping late when you have a small baby—certainly not if you're breast-feeding—so don't get behind on sleep. Fatigue will shatter your cheerfulness faster than anything.

Socializing with a baby

Babies are usually far more adaptable than toddlers when it comes to tagging along. They will generally feed easily and fall asleep happily when they're ready, and you can simply take your sleeping baby home with you. Here are a few pointers to get the best out of socializing as a family.

• A sling or baby carrier allows you to easily move around at a social gathering with your baby.

• Don't stay out too late if you're not getting much sleep. It may take weeks to catch up on sleep you miss between when your baby drops off and when you get home to bed.

• Don't take your baby into smoky or excessively noisy places.

• If you're taking a taxi or sharing a friend's car, don't drop your safety standards. Your baby still needs a proper car seat with a three-point seat belt.

Using affirmations

You can stay cheerful by using positive affirmations. These are phrases you repeat to yourself frequently, and they work on a subconscious level, influencing your emotions. If you keep saying to yourself, "I am relaxed," after a few days you will notice that you really

do feel more relaxed.

Affirmations need to be strong and positive, with no room for doubt. It's no good saying, "I will feel relaxed," or "I'm a bit relaxed." It has to be clear, and it has to be now. Here are some positive affirmations to use when you have a young baby and need help to stay cheerful:

- "I am happy."
- "I am enjoying motherhood."
- "I am relaxed."
- "I am loved."
- "I am appreciated."

Pick the one that suits you, or write a personal affirmation to satisfy your own need. Repeat your affirmation frequently. Say it to yourself twenty times when you first wake up, and throughout the day. Write it on notes and stick them on the bathroom mirror, the refrigerator, and the front door. Repeat it when you go to bed at night. Keep saying it and before long you'll notice a real difference.

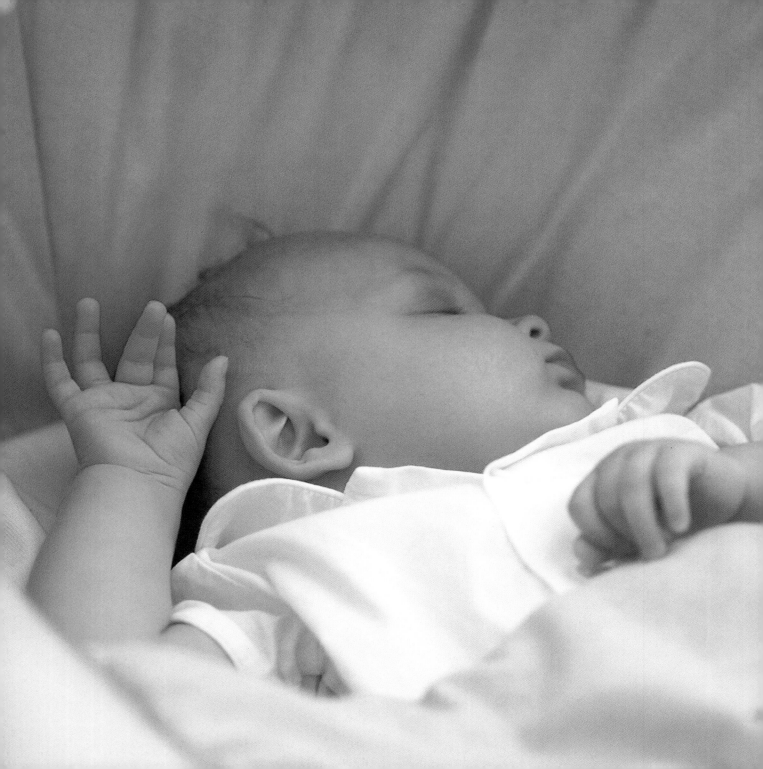

7

Welcome

to the

world

Getting everything ready

Remember yourself

As well as the list of things the doctor will have given you for your hospital bag, consider what else you might want after you've given birth. The process can be exhausting, and you might like to have a package of your favorite cookies or some chocolate with you. (If you can't reward yourself now, when can you?)

If you have a favorite comfortable nightgown or other piece of clothing, you might want this to change into (it must open in the front if you're intending to breast-feed). Or you may want to take a luxury soap or shampoo.

If you plan to give birth at home, you will still want certain things around you, so get them ready in advance to make it easier for yourself when the time comes. Also, there's always the possibility you may have to transfer to the hospital, and it's far simpler to grab a bag that you've already packed.

The better prepared you are for the new baby, the easier the first few weeks will be.

As the date you're due to give birth approaches, you become increasingly excited and impatient. Late pregnancy isn't the most comfortable time, and the anticipation of the birth can make it harder to bear. One of the most useful and satisfying ways to get through this time is to get everything ready for your baby's arrival. Not only that, but as you won't have much time after the birth, now is the ideal time to do everything that you can to make your life easier in the first couple of weeks.

It's good to have the essentials ready by the time you're thirty-six weeks pregnant. Natural gestation in humans is actually anywhere between thirty-six and forty-two weeks, so from thirty-six weeks onward, your baby is technically at full term and could easily arrive.

First things first

There are certain things you'll need for your baby the moment she's born. There's not a lot that small babies need to have, but their basic needs must be covered. Make sure all the following things are ready in the hospital

bag or in the room in which you plan to give birth:
- Diapers
- Baby clothes
- Blankets

If you're going to bottle-feed, you also need:
- Bottles and nipples
- Formula
- Sterilizer

What needs to be ready

You'll enjoy putting the finishing touches to the nursery now and perhaps acquiring a few new items to decorate it. If you're planning to use the crib from the start, get the sheets and other bedding on it now. It may not seem like much, but you'll be glad it's done when the baby arrives. You're not going to feel like making up a bed when you've just given birth.

Likewise, make sure that you've assembled any equipment such as night-lights and mobiles, and that everything is in working order. Again, it'll be harder than you might think to find the time or energy for it immediately after the birth. Other

Getting baby clothes ready is not only necessary but also great fun.

equipment you'll need from the first day or two includes:

- Moses basket or cradle
- Stroller
- Car seat
- Baby bath (plus towels and shampoo)

Make sure that these are ready and that you know how they work. You won't enjoy trying to figure out how the car seat fits when you're still exhausted from the birth and the baby's actually in it, so have a trial run beforehand. The same goes for the stroller, especially if you need to figure out how it folds and unfolds or how the rain cover fits on.

Be prepared

Parents say that having your first baby turns your world upside down, and they're not exaggerating. You feel as if you've been teleported out of one life and into a completely new existence. Having a newborn baby is absolutely nothing like being pregnant. After months of being told to look after yourself and get plenty of rest, all the focus is suddenly on the baby's needs and not yours.

Some babies sleep all through the night from the moment they're born. Most don't. In fact, some babies seem to hardly sleep at all, especially those that are very hungry. You may get as little as three or four hours' sleep a night and not necessarily all at once. That's usually on top of one or more missed nights while you were in labor.

There's not a lot you can do about this if it happens, although there will be plenty of professional advice from medical staff on how to minimize the problems. With help, you'll still thoroughly enjoy your new baby's first few weeks. The important thing is to recognize that severely sleepless nights are a possibility, so that it doesn't catch you completely unaware. Severe lack of sleep can be depressing at times, but for the vast majority of new mothers, the baby is more than worth it and they don't begrudge the sleepless nights. The few tearful days are more than made up for by the joy of having a new baby.

It's important, too, that you realize that it doesn't last forever—you won't have months of sleep deprivation ahead of you. Things improve steadily from the first couple of days, and by six weeks you should notice a significant improvement. By three months your baby should have settled into a manageable pattern. You may still be giving a feeding in the night and you won't get to sleep late, but you should be coping fine and enjoying parenthood.

Overdue baby

One of the most frustrating things that can happen is that your baby doesn't arrive by the due date. This date is obviously only a rough guide, but nevertheless it's the date you've fixed your sights on for months. When you're overdue, especially by more than a few days, it can be hard to cope.

There is a tendency to spend your time waiting for that first sign of impending labor. You're eager to meet your baby face-to-face, and when the meeting is delayed, it can be frustrating and upsetting.

What's more, your social calendar is probably empty. You thought you were going to have a baby by now, so you hadn't made any plans. It's a tough time,

but these suggestions might help:
• Do your best to keep busy with things you can drop at a moment's notice or carry on with after the baby is born (like reading a good book). Don't launch into a project that will leave you frustrated if you can't finish it when the baby arrives.
• Don't travel too far from home or the hospital. Apart from unavoidable commitments such as work, it's best if you and your partner don't travel too far apart. That way, anytime you call, your partner can be there quickly.
• If you have a cell phone, keep it with you all the time for emergency use (but remember that it's not a good idea to use it too much while you're pregnant).
• Book as many social dates as you like into your calendar. Just make sure they are all local and not too tiring, and all with friends who understand that you may drop out at the very last moment (without even calling to warn them). Understanding friends and family won't have a problem with this.

Above all, don't be concerned if you go over term. It can happen to anyone, even if you've had previous babies early or on time. It's far easier to cope with if you've anticipated the possibility than if you assumed that your baby wouldn't be late.

Plan your schedule carefully in case your baby is late.

A welcoming birth

The first few minutes

Your baby's first few moments after she leaves the sanctuary of the womb will either reassure her that this strange new world is still safe or leave her frightened and unhappy. You obviously want to make sure that the former is the case. So, apart from setting the atmosphere, what will help to reassure your baby that birth is a happy experience? Here are the most valuable things you can give your baby in those first minutes:

- The sound of your voice, familiar and reassuring
- The warmth of being held close
- The touch of skin against skin
- The smell of your body, which she will recognize
- The taste of warm milk, which she will instinctively want after the effort of the birth

The moment of birth is one of the most magical and memorable things you will ever experience. Despite how it may feel at the time, the closing stages of labor and the first few minutes after the birth don't last for long. If you want your baby to have a safe, warm, and peaceful arrival into the world, this is the time to create the conditions and the atmosphere that will contribute to it.

Creating the best atmosphere

In the last few decades, the traditional Western birth has involved being born into a stark, busy, brightly lit hospital room. The light, the space, and the busy atmosphere could hardly be more different from the conditions the baby has been used to for the last few months. In many other cultures, however, babies are born into quiet, dark rooms, as similar as possible to the womb itself. This is obviously far less of a shock for the baby, which is why there is a growing trend in the West to adopt the same approach.

Most hospitals now do as much as they can to encourage you to choose your own birth conditions. Some even place a special emphasis on creating a peaceful, welcoming atmosphere by providing a choice of music for you. There are several ways you can appeal to your new baby's senses with relaxing or familiar conditions, making her entry into the world as happy and as welcoming as possible. Here are some suggestions:

LIGHTS: Your baby is emerging from a dark world into which only a little light filters. So it is far more familiar for her to be born into a dimly lit room. You can light candles or have a dimmer switch turned down as low as possible. As long as there are no complications, it is perfectly possible for the medical staff to manage in low light levels.

SOUND: Although your baby has been muffled inside the womb, sounds have still filtered through. The sound of your voice and those of close family will have become familiar, as will any music that you listened to regularly during pregnancy. Both you and your baby will be calmed by gentle music playing during the birth.

TOUCH: Your baby has never been alone without the sensation of your body surrounding her. As soon as she is born, one of the most comforting things you can do is to hold her so that she knows she is still safe in this new world.

A home birth is usually perfectly safe if it is planned properly and you can get to a hospital quickly if you need to.

MOOD: Babies are deeply sensitive to mood and emotions both inside the womb and after birth. Your baby will respond to a peaceful, gentle atmosphere far more happily than to a frenetic, hurried room full of scurrying people.

Home birth

The vast majority of women choose to give birth in the hospital these days. However, studies indicate that home births are safe for most women, as long as they are planned and there is a hospital within reach in case it's needed. If you want a home birth and your doctor doesn't advise against it, you will benefit greatly from the experience.

Giving birth at home means you are in familiar surroundings with all your things around you, from your favorite pillow to your own brand of juice. Your baby will be born into her own home,

Involving both parents

Although a baby is carried inside her mother's body for nine months, she is as much a product of her father, so the father has as much of a stake in the birth (albeit less of the discomfort). Having both parents present is ideal; the father can give support and encouragement during the labor, as well as practical help such as massage. Although many first-time fathers balk at the prospect before the birth, almost all report that they wouldn't have missed the experience for anything.

As soon as the baby is born, the mother usually holds her. But if she has difficulty doing this, the father is the next best person. The baby will respond positively to his familiar voice and enjoy being held. Skin-to-skin contact is important, so it's a good thing if the father takes off his shirt before holding his new baby.

After a few minutes, the medical staff will want to weigh and check the baby, and dress or wrap her up warmly. They generally do this while the mother is getting cleaned up and into bed ready to hold her baby again and to feed her. The father can hold her and be with her while she is weighed, and dress her before handing her to the mother. This kind of involvement right after the birth is great for both baby and father, and gets the bonding off to a good start.

with a comforting Moses basket rather than a hospital crib, and her family around it.

You will feel far more in control of the process than you might in a hospital, and the medical staff will recognize that this is your home territory. The health professionals who attend home births are almost invariably in favor of minimal intervention, so you should have as natural a birth as you want. The chief disadvantage is that if you decide you want strong pain relief such as an epidural, you'll have to transfer to a hospital.

If you have older children, a home birth is particularly good. Rather than leaving them for a couple of days and then returning with a new baby in tow, you'll be there all the time (although they will still need to be cared for by close family or friends). What's more, you will have been through the experience of giving birth before; home births are especially relaxing for second or subsequent babies if your previous deliveries have been straightforward.

Some women will advise you against a home birth, because it's not something they would choose to do themselves. If you plan to deliver at home, be prepared for plenty of comments along the lines of, "How brave!" Don't let this undermine you. If a home birth is what you want and the health professionals give you the green light, then go for it.

Water births

Your baby has spent its entire life so far underwater, so what could be more natural and familiar than to emerge into water? She won't need to breathe as long as the umbilical cord is still working, and won't start breathing automatically until the air touches her face. She can therefore safely be born in a birthing pool.

A water birth is an option if you aren't using drugs for pain relief (water births are contraindicated with most such drugs), and the water itself acts as a natural painkiller. Many mothers have excellent experiences with water births, whether the baby is born underwater or the mother stands or gets out of the pool just before the birth. Some hospital maternity units have birthing pools, and you can rent your own if you're planning a home birth.

The key points usually cited in favor of water births are:

• The buoyancy of being in the water, which means you don't have to support your own weight

For some women, giving birth in water offers natural pain relief and creates a relaxing environment for the baby to be born into.

- The warmth
- The natural pain relief

Being adaptable

You've had months to think about the birth, and no doubt you'll have come up with a clear picture of the birth you would like for you and your baby. Maybe you want to be in a hospital birthing pool, or perhaps at home in your own bed. You may have decided that you want to avoid using pain medicine or that you want to be listening to your favorite piece of music.

If your wishes are reasonable and safe, there is every chance that you'll get the birth you want. But things don't always work out as planned, and it's a good idea to think through the alternatives. If you have your heart set on a particular kind of delivery and it doesn't happen, the whole experience may be spoiled for you. However, if you've prepared emotionally and in practical terms for an alternative, it will be easier for you to adapt and still get the most from the birth experience.

If you're planning a home birth, be aware that there may be complications that necessitate going to the hospital. So visit your local maternity ward and find out where you would give birth if this happened. Visualize having a hospital birth instead. Pack a hospital bag just in case, including anything you might want such as candles or CDs.

If you want a water birth, find out what will happen if the birthing pool is unavailable or if complications make it unsuitable. Learn about epidurals in case you need one after all. Ask about cesarians just in case—you may not have time to ask questions if you need an emergency cesarean section.

The aim is not to be negative about everything that could go wrong, but to find a positive way of looking at all these alternatives (which will only come into play for the good of you and your baby). Then if they do happen, you'll still be able to enjoy the experience. If you're prepared for anything, nothing will take you by surprise.

Asserting your baby's rights

The medical staff who attend you at the birth are there to help and will almost certainly do a great job. However, their idea of an ideal birth may not be the same as yours. Especially in hospitals, they can be so used to a clinical environment with a predisposition to medical intervention that you may have to be very clear about what you want.

This is your labor and if you feel strongly that, for example, you want low lighting, or don't want the cord cut for the first few minutes, then say so. Most health professionals will bend over backward to cooperate, but a few are set in their ways and you may need to be polite but firm. Here are some pointers:
• Draw up a birth plan well in advance so your wishes are clear and unambiguous.
• You are not going to be in your best state for rational argument; this is one of those times when your partner can be a big help.
• While you and your partner may need

Holding and cuddling the baby soon after birth helps your partner to create a strong bond right away.

to be assertive, it's not worth falling out with your doctor. This is not an occasion to spoil with unpleasantness unless the issue at stake is more important than the atmosphere in the delivery room. If you really feel this is not the doctor for you, ask for someone else if you can.

• Recognize that there may be a legitimate reason why your doctor can't do what you want, but ask him or her to explain the reason(s) clearly.

Help and privacy

Taking care of the family

If you have other children, they will be a primary concern. Someone will have to look after them while you're in labor. The experience is likely to be strange to them, so they should be with someone familiar whom they like. Here are a few pointers to help you choose a suitable caregiver:

• Bear in mind that you need to be able to call on someone day or night, without warning.

• Even if you plan a home birth, have backup care arranged for your children in case you have to go into a hospital.

• Even if you have a home birth that goes according to plan, your partner should ideally be with you and the baby rather than looking after other children.

• Prepare detailed instructions for the twenty-four hours and needs to be able to feed and clothe the children, get them to school, look after pets, and do other essential chores.

• The best option might be to have more than one caregiver on standby. You might call one person during the day and another if you go into labor at night.

• Explain to your children what you've planned, including contingency plans, so they know what to expect.

When you give birth, and for the first few days afterward, you'll be tired and uncomfortable. The more help you can get, the better. For a start, you'll need a supportive birth partner, preferably the baby's father, who can attend prenatal classes with you so they are prepared.

A birth partner can encourage you, support you, massage your back, and fetch you glasses of water, tissues, or anything else you might need. Having a partner present is also extremely useful during the moments around the actual birth. A doctor's or nurse's instructions can seem very distant, but a partner keeping eye contact with you and repeating them—"Push!" "Breathe!" "Don't push!"—means that they sink in and you can act on them.

Doula help

Whether or not you have a partner with you for the birth, some women now opt to employ extra assistance in the form of a doula. A doula is a nonmedical, certified childbirth assistant who attends your labor and helps you through it. Unlike the hospital staff who come and go according to their shifts, and whom you probably won't have met before, a doula gets to know you before the birth and can stay throughout it.

This has all sorts of advantages. For a start, you know your doula and presumably like her or you wouldn't have hired her. She knows what kind of labor you want and can help to make sure you get it. Studies have shown that women who have a doula present during childbirth have shorter labors with fewer complications and get less stressed by the experience.

Your doula should get to know both you and your partner during pregnancy, so that all three of you can discuss the kind of labor you want. A good doula won't try to supplant your partner but will work with both of you, keeping out of the way at those moments when you and your partner want some privacy during the labor.

You can find a doula by asking friends or your doctor for recommendations.

Help at home

You may have just given birth, but the house still has to be run, especially if you have other children. There are meals to cook, laundry to wash, and shopping to do. You can get away with a couple of weeks without cleaning or other nonessentials, but some things really do have to be done.

Breast-feeding your baby can be hard work since you can't share this with anyone, but it is usually a deeply rewarding experience and excellent time out from a busy life.

Looking after older children

If you have an older child or children, things are going to be a bit different for them for a while. As well as wanting to avoid feelings of jealousy, you also want your older children to feel secure and loved. There are steps you and those who are helping you can take in the first few days to encourage this.

- Make sure you give your older children as much love and positive encouragement as you can, even if you can't spare them much time or energy.
- Try not to snap every time they touch the baby, but grit your teeth (if necessary) and teach them how to be gentle.
- Whoever is looking after the older child—father, grandparent, friend—shouldn't relax the normal rules. Rules and boundaries are vital components of young children's security. When their world is already worryingly changed, the last thing they need is for the boundaries to be removed as well.
- Encourage visitors to bring a small gift for older children if they're bringing one for the baby.
- If you feel you can, ask them to greet the older children first rather than rushing past them to see the baby. Encourage them also to chat to the older children about themselves as well as talking to you about the baby.

On top of that, there's all the activity generated by a new baby—bathing her, changing her, feeding her, sterilizing bottles—all of which are probably new skills if this is your first baby. If your partner doesn't get time off work (and even if he does), he can't do everything, along with looking after you. He may well already have lost a night's sleep or more during the labor.

Face it, you need help. The question is, who are you going to ask? Think carefully, because you're going to be at your weakest and most vulnerable. If you don't get along with your in-laws at the best of times, this isn't the time to invite them to stay. Maybe a week of take-out and no clean laundry would be preferable. If help is offered, you and your partner may need to be assertive; if you're not, you could regret it.

Make sure you ask for help from people you are happy to have around at this vulnerable time, or who are local enough that you can ask them to drop in for a couple of hours a day rather than come for a prolonged stay. If people want to feel involved and you worry that a refusal might hurt their feelings, ask for some other kind of help. The following are areas in which other people's help could be invaluable:

- Picking up your laundry a couple of times and doing it for you.
- Watching your older children for a couple of hours after school.
- Cooking a week's worth of meals to put in your freezer.
- Doing any essential shopping for you.
- Allowing you to stay with them in a few weeks' time instead, when you'll need a break from the chores.

There'll be no shortage of offers of help, and you probably ought to accept most of them. One of the best ways friends can help is to visit you in the evening and bring dinner with them (don't let them cook it for you and then leave you with all the dirty dishes). This means they get to see the baby, and you get a healthy meal without you or your partner having to cook.

Another option for help is to hire what is known as a postpartum doula, who will help look after the baby, cook for you, do light housework, and generally ease the burden of caring for a new baby and running a house before you're fully fit. They will usually stay for up to a month, and will give you welcome opportunities to catch up on sleep, rest, recuperate, and get back in shape.

Maintaining your privacy

Everyone loves visiting a new baby. You're likely to be flooded with visitors—friends, family, neighbors—not to mention the standard visits from health professionals. If you're in a hospital with restricted visiting hours, you might find yourself very grateful for it. But what if you're not?

Your friends and family mean well, but they may not realize how exhausted you are or how many other visitors you've had. Whether you're in the hospital or have just returned home, you may well find that all you want is some time alone with your baby and your partner, and any other children you have.

The best way to deal with this is in advance. Let all your family and friends know that you would love them to visit, but only during certain times. Explain that you are exhausted, and you'll be sleeping every chance you get. Make sure you offer people a time when they can visit, so that they don't feel excluded.

If you start making exceptions to this rule, other people may feel put out that they weren't treated as exceptions, too. Since the days after birth are no time to be patching up blossoming family feuds, your best bet is to make no exceptions at all, except, of course, for your partner and the baby's big brothers or sisters.

Try to encourage visitors to bring a gift for older children as well as a gift for the baby.

Grandparents can provide invaluable support with a new baby and help to care for older brothers and sisters.

Choosing a name

Your baby's name will become an intrinsic part of her individual identity.

Deciding what to name your baby is one of the exciting aspects of pregnancy. It can be great fun going through lists of names. Sooner or later, though, you have to make a final choice, and that can be difficult.

What starts out as just one more name on a list will eventually become an intrinsic part of your child's identity and self-image. Like it or not, names give away a great deal about people—or at least about their backgrounds and the kind of family they have. People will judge your child differently throughout life depending on whether she's a Sabrina or a Sue. A boy named William may be treated differently from a boy named Wayne.

You may have strong views on whether you want your child to have a common name or an unusual one, and there obviously is no right or wrong. You simply need to be aware that when you name your baby you are giving her far more than a collection of letters to identify her by. You are giving her an image that will be with her for life.

Only you can know what names you like. But here are some pointers to help you choose wisely:

• Don't try to pressure your partner into using a name he really dislikes. Keep looking until you find some common ground, even if there's an element of compromise for both of you.

• If you and your partner are happy with the name, that's what's important. You can canvas as many opinions as you like, but your opinion is the only one that really matters.

• If you have older children, involve them in the decision but let them know that everyone has to agree and they may not get their first choice of name.

• If you prefer unusual names, try to pick one that your child can easily shorten to something more common if she wants to.

• Bear in mind that boys with very unusual first names are more likely to be picked on at school, according to research. This seems to be less of an issue for girls.

• If you're unsure whether to go for an unusual name, take into account the last name; it generally works to pair a common first name with an unusual last name and vice versa.

• Avoid names that are in fashion for a short time, such as those of sports heroes or pop stars.

• Avoid names of ex-boyfriends and

girlfriends, even if the choice is purely coincidental, unless you have an extremely enlightened partner.

- Think carefully before you give a child a descriptive name—if she doesn't live up to it, it could be a burden.
- If you come from a different cultural background than the country you live in, think about whether you want to give your child a name from your culture or that of your adopted country. Perhaps you could find a name from your culture that sounds like a name from the country you live in.
- Think about the initials.
- Consider what nicknames friends will inevitably use. If you don't like them, perhaps choose a different name.
- Say the name out loud, together with the last name, and see how it sounds. A long first name often works better with a short last name, and vice versa.

Family names

Parents often like to use names of someone in the family. There might be a traditional family name, or you might want to name your baby after a family member. If you both agree and your families are happy, this is no problem. But suppose one of you hates the name,

or one side of the family is offended that they weren't included, too—what do you do? The following suggestions might help:

- If you don't like the name, you could use it as a middle name rather than a first name.
- You may be able to give the child a name you're not keen on and then shorten it to one you like. For example, you might not like the name Jonathan, but Jon would be fine.
- If you take a name from one side of the family, you can generally avoid offense by taking a name from the other side as well. It may be best not to give one name precedence, but to use both as middle names.
- Take a name from one side of the family only, and tell the other side of the family that your next child will be named after them.
- If you really don't want to use a particular name despite the pressure or want to use it as a middle name and not a first name, you could wait until the baby is born and then say, "We were thinking of using the name, but he just didn't look like a Rutherford."
- Don't tell your family what names you are considering. Wait until you have decided and after the baby is born.

Hidden meanings

Almost all names have a meaning, according to the language or place from which they originate. Andrew, for example, means "strong and manly" (from the Greek), and Emily is a Teutonic name meaning "hard-working."

You may want to choose a name for your child that means something relevant and special to you, or which indicates a quality you want your child to possess.

For example, you might want to call a girl Larissa, from the Greek meaning "happy girl." If a boy has been very active during pregnancy, you might name him Gale, which means "lively one" in Celtic.

Bringing the baby home

Ask for help

If you lack confidence about looking after your baby at home, that's perfectly normal. Just remember that the only essentials are to keep your baby warm, well fed, and physically safe. Everything else can wait until you are ready to cope with it. It doesn't matter if the baby is in the same clothes for twenty-four hours (so long as you change her diaper). If you're nervous about bathing the baby, wait until there's someone there who can help.

Don't be afraid to ask for help from health professionals, friends, neighbors, or family who have had babies of their own. They'll be pleased to help, and you'll get the hang of it all faster than you think. Within a week or so you'll be changing and bathing the baby like an old hand.

Bringing your baby back to the sanctuary of her own home is a moving experience.

Giving birth in the hospital means you are surrounded by experts who will help you look after the baby and give you good advice on everything from feeding and bathing your baby to helping your own body repair itself. Going home with the baby can be a nerve-racking experience, as you suddenly feel your safety net has been taken away and you're on your own.

The more you can do to make sure your homecoming is an occasion for happiness rather than worry, the better. Not only are you returning home, but you are also introducing your baby to the home that will be her security and sanctuary for the future.

At least part of you will almost certainly be very happy to get home. No more hospital food, other people's babies crying, or impersonal baby equipment. You'll be back in your own bed, with your own favorite foods in the kitchen, and, if you have them, back with your other children. And you can finally add the last essential ingredient—the baby—to that lovingly prepared nursery.

The more you have prepared yourself for this in advance, the more confident and happy you will feel. If you've read the books, been to the classes, and asked lots of questions at the hospital, you will be more than capable of looking after your baby. The more your partner can help, the better. Not only will you feel supported, but he will feel more involved and will recognize the importance of his own role. If at least one of you is thoroughly familiar with the workings of the car seat, the sterilizer, the sling, the baby monitor, and any other equipment, so much the better. This is a good opportunity for your partner to take the lead. You won't feel much like struggling with seat belts or folding strollers right now, so let them take charge of the equipment.

You may feel so drained that you don't want any visitors for a couple of days, and it's entirely reasonable to ask other people to leave you alone. It may be tough to keep people away from the baby for too long, but forty-eight hours to yourself is a great settling-in period when you and your immediate family can really enjoy being together and starting to find a new routine.

The better you've prepared for this moment, the more likely you will be able to enjoy it. After months of planning and anticipation, there are few feelings that beat walking through the front door of your own personal sanctuary as a family.

Index

Acknowledgments

The publisher wishes to thank the following for supplying the photographs for this book.

© Bubbles: pages 19 (Claire Paxton), 20 (Chris Rout), 22 (Ian West), 31 *top* (Loisjoy Thurstan) *bottom* (Loisjoy Thurstan), 36 (Lucy Tizard), 37 (Lucy Tizard), 38 (Loisjoy Thurstun), 45 (Loisjoy Thurstun), 49 (Angela Hampton), 50 (Lucy Tizard), 55 *left* (Loisjoy Thurstun) *right* (Lucy Tizard), 61 (Julie Fisher), 71 (Jennie Woodcock), 81 (Loisjoy Thurstun).

© Getty Images: pages 2–3 (Tosca Radigonda), 23 (Owen Franken), 46 (Eyewire), 56 (Britt Erlanson), 58 (Ross Whitaker), 85 (Kindra Clineff), 101 (Taxi), 121 *main* (Sue Ann Miller) *inset* (Eyewire).

©Mother and Baby: pages 16 (Paul Mitchell), 17(Paul Mitchell), 21 (Ian Hooton), 28 (Ruth Jenkinson), 42 (Ian Hooton), 57 (Ian Hooton), 76 (Ian Hooton), 79 (Ian Hooton), 82 (Ian Hooton), 83 (Ian Hooton), 88 (Ian Hooton), 89 (Ian Hooton), 92 (Ian Hooton), 95 (Ruth Jenkinson), 103 (Ruth Jenkinson), 105 (Verity Wellstead), 110 (Ian Hooton), 111 (Sean Knox), 113 (Eddie Lawrence), 115 (Moose Azim), 119 (Paul Mitchell), 122 (Ian Hooton), 125 (Ian Hooton).

© Science Photo Library: pages 117 (Tracy Dominey).

© The White Company: pages 32, 34, 108.

© Wigwamkids: pages 4, 11, 29, 35, 40, 51, 109, 123.